Teaching Writing to Second Language Learners

Teaching Writing to Second Language Learners

Dr Riaz Hassan

iUniverse, Inc.
New York   Bloomington

iUniverse books may be ordered through booksellers or by contacting:

iUniverse
1663 Liberty Drive
Bloomington, IN 47403
www.iuniverse.com
1-800-Authors (1-800-288-4677)

Because of the dynamic nature of the Internet, any Web addresses or
links contained in this book may have changed since publication and may
no longer be valid. The views expressed in this work are solely those of
the author and do not necessarily reflect the views of the publisher, and
the publisher hereby disclaims any responsibility for them.

ISBN: 978-1-4401-4186-7 (sc)
ISBN: 978-1-4401-4185-0 (ebook)

Library of Congress Control Number: 2009927532

Printed in the United States of America

iUniverse rev. date: 04/24/2009

Table of Contents

Chapter One

The broad subject of this work is teaching writing in English in a third-world setting. It is intended mainly for Pakistani speakers and users of English. It might also be relevant to some parts of South Asian countries such as India, especially among Indian speakers who live north of the River Cauveri. It might even be relevant to other third-world countries that wake up to the developmental advantages of knowing a world language such as English. The focus of this study is primarily on post-graduate writing in English. It is not an error-analysis, though some effort will be made to discover deviant patterns in writing. Some general approaches to writing are discussed with a view to help mature students to improve their writing skills, and teachers to assist them in the process.

The author has explored some aspects of writing and the failure to develop adequate writing skills in English in Pakistan. The primary failure can be traced to the school system. English is begun rather late in the vernacular stream, and students in that stream labour under disadvantages compared with students in the English-medium stream all the way through, especially in subjects that require large inputs of written English.

While there is a great mass of literature about writing and literacy in general in the English-speaking world, not much can be found about the situation in Pakistan. Dr. Robert Baumgardner and other writers working with him have pointed out quite a few characteristics and deviations (*The English Language in Pakistan*, ed., R.Baumgardner, OUP Karachi, 1993) and so has Dr. Tariq Rahman (*Pakistani English*, Vanguard, Islamabad, 1990). The author also did some inadequate work in this field in the seventies and eighties. There are regular deviations, frequent and persistent enough to suggest that Pakistani dialects of English are deeply etched and reasonably stable. This raises the question of whether to accept them as valid variants of English, to teach them as such, and to evaluate Pakistani students in accordance with them (or one of them), as we hear some Indians are trying to do across the border, or whether to insist on an international standard of English. Should the drift be accepted as *a fait accompli?* Pakistani English has gone its own way despite a lot of governmental and educational effort to stop the drift. Pakistanis write this kind of English, regardless of anything one might do to halt or reverse it. It seems rather mean, to say the least, to expose them to one kind of English for several years, and then to penalise them because they cannot operate very well in another, yet this happens regularly. The failure rate in English is still very high.

Some of these questions are explored here. The author is of the opinion that Standard English, if such a thing exists and can be defined reasonably well, should continue to be taught, especially for writing. Spoken accents do not matter very much provided they remain within an acceptable band of comprehensibility. Australian, New Zealand, South African, Irish, Canadian, American and British people, all native speakers in the sense that English is used constantly at all levels and for all purposes within their societies, have distinct ways (and distinct ways within those ways) of speaking the language, but their written English, or at least their *formal* written English, tends to be fairly uniform apart from variations in spelling and idiom which are soon accommodated.

The factors that lead to deviations in *spoken* Pakistani English are well known--mother-tongue interference, transliteration, different sounds and differences in the *production* of related sounds in the two languages, different approaches, different cultural perceptions, different stress and intonation patterns and difficulties with the non-phonetic nature of English orthography. But one feels that writing should be brought much more in line with international standards than it is today.

One cannot blame Pakistani students for their failure to master the medium. They are exposed to large amounts of deviant writing in newspapers, television announcements, commercial advertising and public notices, apart from their unhappy experiences at school. There is no escaping the fact that the situation is not good. The question is, can something be done at the college or university end, what some people might call the *wrong* end, to improve the situation?

The author's dissatisfaction with the written output of senior students in Pakistan is behind the following effort. It is compounded by a second problem, namely that the teacher's daily chore of proof-reading, marking and correcting assignments does not seem to result in any visible improvement. Second drafts are often as bad as first ones. As often, they repeat the mistakes corrected so painstakingly in the first one. Students remain reluctant to write, and write badly when they are cajoled or bullied into doing so.

Some time ago the author attempted to change his approach and to apply more recent ideas about writing to see if any difference could be made. Basically, it consisted of improving the emotional atmosphere of the writing class so that students did not feel threatened by the possibility of censure, failure or ridicule. Output of any kind, on any subject related to what was being discussed in class, was encouraged, even if the language was faulty. This was done in rare moments found when a little experimentation became possible during the otherwise overwhelming demands of the curriculum.

The response in the beginning was slow. Some students still preferred to hand in assignments taken with the minimum of personal editing from other sources. These were returned, almost without comment. Only those that in the opinion of the researcher represented real attempts at language production were considered. Excerpts from student writing are included in this thesis. Two of them are by the same student, with a gap of ten days between them.

Later, some focus was put on matters of spelling, grammar and punctuation, but not in the traditional way. Signs of improvement were observed in some cases, and these prompted the writing of this work. The mere fact that writing could be seen as a learnable skill and not a simple reflex of reading seemed to help. However, too many factors operate in the skills of writing to suggest that dramatic improvements will come about immediately. At best a teacher will succeed in setting his students on the path, so that they can continue to explore things for themselves. In the final analysis, all learning is self-learning.

This work attempts to discover two things: (a) operative factors in the process of writing, and (b) why, after years of learning English, older Pakistani students continue to stutter in their writing chores and endlessly repeat mistakes of a certain kind. It also attempts to understand the effects of literacy in *one* language, and of adequate literacy in *two* languages, on the individual and on society in general, and suggests what might be done to help young adults so that they are not handicapped in their studies or professions. The question of whether literacy in one language can be used to develop it in another is also raised.

Finally, it recommends areas in which controlled research may be done. The methodology of this kind of research would be rather different from the modest approach adopted here. What appears here is largely what the author has gathered from books and articles written about the skills of writing, all fitted into a framework of direct observation rejected or validated informally over a number of years. However, mounting and conducting surveys, planning and setting up experiments, controlling settings, collecting information, tabulating results, interpreting data and validating and revising findings necessitate much more by way of formal inputs of time, movement, expertise and money, preferably on a continuous basis.

In the final chapter the author has made a plea for setting up at least one research centre for linguistic studies in the country. He has suggested that the first one be located at the National University of Modern Languages in Islamabad. Good access to modern documents all round the world is a pre-requisite, with a well organised materials research and development centre willing to share its resources with other agencies at home or abroad. In the fullness of time laboratory sections could be added, with machines to show sound oscillations, chronometers to measure reaction times, mini language laboratories, measuring tools, machines for enhancing reading speed, recording cells and equipment, computers with internet connections, printers and other machines as they are developed, or as required.

The study of English is caught and restricted by the constraints of a certain kind of syllabus planning which was decided for schools in the local system decades ago. The fact that it is not working well is confirmed by the rising number of parents, who, at considerable cost, insist on sending their children to English-medium schools. The happy few who have tons of money prefer to send them abroad, because even these schools do not achieve much.

Decades later, no decision-making agency has seen fit to question or change the base plan. It is not a matter of money or teacher resources. It is a matter of language, especially of the English language. The nation cannot afford *not* to find the resources for improving the situation. The cost in real terms, money, wasted man-hours, student inefficiency, overwhelming failure rates, low standards, flagging international ratings, poor output in research and widespread linguistic despondency, is a heavy one. However, this is not to suggest that changing the system will automatically improve everything. Too many interlocking factors conspire to work against the ideal of excellence. Perhaps at this stage it is more practical to work for the ideal of adequacy. Some changes are due, even for that.

The way the English language is going, not only in Pakistan but everywhere in the world, its present status within the country must be reassessed. Its future status must also be anticipated. The ability to acquire advanced knowledge through it with some efficiency and certitude, and to write in it with some competence and confidence, is already extremely important for young Pakistanis, more so today than when the writer was a young man. This importance will increase in coming years.

Chapter Two

Learning to Write: The Premises of Writing

The Situation

The bulk of teaching material in writing focuses on the school-going child. The assumption made by educational planners is that by the time he gets to college he will be proficient in writing. Sadly, as any university teacher in Pakistan will testify, this assumption cannot be endorsed. In the real world of secondary and higher education, teachers are forced to contend with reams of badly written assignments. Most of the average teacher's time is spent 'correcting' faulty scripts, in making little red or green marks like 'sp' for *spelling* or 'gr' for *grammar* all over page after page of written material in the hope that his students will correct themselves as they go along, but finding to his dismay with the next assignment that nothing has been corrected, nothing achieved. The ideal *of* teacher-student discussion and interaction at a high level of scholarship is remote indeed.

Oracy and Literacy

Writing is the most intractable of the four skills. This might be because it is the least natural in the sense that it has to be learnt, i.e. the process usually starts late, and it may not have the child's natural language ability behind it. A study of psycholinguistics confirms what has always been known, that infants learn the 'oracy' skills (listening and speaking) of the language spoken by the people who matter to them, regardless of instruction, pointing to the existence of some kind of natural language ability in very young human beings (1), at least for listening and speaking. This ability may be wide enough to accommodate a second language in a multi-lingual setting, provided the child's exposure is early and consistent enough (2).

Nativists argue that without this innate ability a child would not be able to acquire a language, and they are clearly right. Equally right are empiricists who say that external inputs are necessary ingredients in the process—after all, a child acquires the language he hears spoken by people around him. Under suitable conditions deaf infants who have not had the natural benefit of sound in the acquisition process readily learn to encode and decode a series of hand and bodily gestures as a substitute for listening and speaking, though they might never develop speaking skills without special training. This is a genuine linguistic achievement through the eyes rather than the ears that reinforces the 'innate ability' hypothesis, the assumption that there is an innate Language Acquisition Device (LAD) or Language Acquisition System (LAS) (3).

However, not all commentators accept this assumption. Samson states that:

> ...Individual humans inherit no 'knowledge of language'... they succeed in mastering the language spoken in their environment only by applying the same general intelligence which they use to grapple with all the other diverse and unpredictable problems that come their way...(4)

Samson's remarks are interesting in that he talks about an 'inherent knowledge' of language rather than an 'inherent ability' to acquire language. This takes the discussion into another domain, almost certainly not what the native theorists have in mind. That people have the physical ability to produce the typical sounds of human language by the descent of the larynx soon after birth, a characteristic not shared by other closely related species, should have clinched the matter. It is that human beings 'can' learn languages, whereas animals cannot, at least not in the same way--and not that human children already 'know' language.

This is reminiscent of the old argument in psychology as to whether there are separate 'faculties' and aptitudes for learning things, such as an aptitude for mathematics or a faculty for learning the piano, or whether there is one central G-factor which radiates through all learning activities. If it is a matter of developed intelligence, an adult ought to be able to learn languages more easily than a child. This is not borne out by observation. Nor does intelligence seem to be a crucial determiner of language ability— 'slow' children also acquire language, though they might never use it as cleverly as 'sharp' children.

Actually, a child's brain works with a great deal of

uncluttered, unconscious energy for the first six or seven years. Thereafter some of its pristine abilities seem to fade and by the age of thirteen or fourteen it is said to lose much of its ability to handle language inputs (5).

Literacy

Some children begin to acquire reading and writing skills quite early, while their brains still have the peculiar energy mentioned earlier. These skills come to them more easily than to those who are introduced to them later, after the age of six or seven. Till recently in Pakistan, English was started in class six, when a child might be anywhere from ten to thirteen years of age, sometimes even older. If the purpose was to make him literate in English, this was probably too late. Even so, whether the process is natural, artificial, or a mixture of both, by the time he got to college as a young man he would have had at least seven years of formal exposure to English, a lot of it in written form. Our higher education entrants are not, or should not be, strangers to the written word in the second language. It is puzzling, therefore, to see so much poorly written English among senior students.

One is entitled to ask if there is an innate ability for the 'literacy' skills of reading and writing as well. It may be argued that if speaking is acquired through listening, then writing should be acquired through reading. The productive skill follows the receptive one. However, if the child's natural, primary perception is aural-oral, his acquisition of the literacy skills of reading and writing is tantamount, almost, to learning his language all over again in a different context, a relatively unnatural one. His 'literacy' perception, when it comes, is without genuine sounds, though there may be some internal vocalisation. Thus it is argued that an individual who has acquired all four skills has therefore learnt the language twice, once naturally from its sounds, and once again artificially from its graphemes.

There are some obvious differences between the two conventions. Oral language is in real time, the feedback is instantaneous, it is confined to audible ranges, it is ephemeral, it relies in large measure on gesture and intonation for meaning, it tends to be short, ejaculatory, redundant and repetitious, it is riddled with ambiguity, it functions within a situational, supportive framework, moves in one direction and is liable to all kinds of misinterpretation. In contrast, written language is not time bound, the feedback might be delayed (or there may be no feedback at all), its range is much wider, it is comparatively static and permanent, it has no semantic support from gesture, intonation, stress or situation, and in concept and organic structure it might be more complex. While written texts can also be misinterpreted (all manifestations of language can), it is usually crafted more carefully. The mere fact that the short-term memory is less taxed in decoding writing makes it less liable to misinterpretation, or so we hope. Once written, it lies there as a permanent record of a man's thoughts and expression. It does not 'move' forward in the way that spoken language does, but lies as a static block of small black marks on a piece of paper. It is open to criticism in a way that evanescent speech is not, and this is a powerful inhibitory factor for many students. This is especially true of the world of academics where near perfection in writing is demanded.

Of course, writing also has many traps. Lacking the support of gesture, intonation, stress, feedback and situation, it is open to misinterpretation in other ways. This is true of all text, but especially true when we try to interpret ancient texts. All languages change in all sorts of ways. Meanings of words change, or develop salience, or slip into obscurity among different connotations of words. Words may even begin to mean the opposite of what they meant when they were first used. Grammar might also change, as we see when we compare modern English with earlier structural forms of the language (5). Situations and cultural expectations also change. One can never be sure when reading old texts that one understands what they mean. Writing can only suggest the spoken word, it cannot duplicate it. Texts derived from oral traditions or sources are even more suspect when they are viewed after even a small lapse of time, let alone decades or centuries later.

No doubt writing started when people felt the need to keep records, perhaps first of all for business contracts and property ownership, but it would be wrong to think of it as a graphemic rendering of speaking only. Its inestimable ability to transmit knowledge from one generation to another must have become apparent very soon. While it can certainly be a written record of speech, it has also gone its own way, because it works on a different set of premises and in a different medium. The oral tradition is still found in small village cultures, but, much more than speech, writing is the glue that holds different eras together in the evolution of great civilisations. The impulse to develop writing systems through pictures, symbols, ideas or sounds probably rests on a need for something reliable to 'fix' agreements and transactions, so that there is no argument or backtracking later. Probably in the beginning, any given small group of people needed only a few scribes and specialists. The vast majority of people would be content to have learnt their language only once, in the way it was naturally meant to be learnt, as a means of communication through aural/oral mechanisms and skills. In a predominantly agrarian setup such as South Asia's, reading might be uncommon, but writing is rare indeed, and the definition of literacy is usually lenient, perhaps asking for little more than an ability to write one's own name.

In any case, by the age of six or seven, a child will have mastered most of his language's basic structures and will have an adequate working vocabulary for the give and take of daily life in his circumscribed world. Krashen tends to the belief that reading is similar to acquiring a second language (6). The word 'acquiring' is used deliberately in the sense of something gained unconsciously, by being immersed in an environment where the language is used continuously, as opposed to 'learning', which may be described as a conscious effort to understand and internalise something. There is some evidence to suggest that the complex skills of reading are helped by innate factors as well, especially if a child is introduced to written texts before the door closes. According to one researcher this door begins to close at about the age of six (7). There is little evidence to support the hypothesis that the complex psychological and motor process called writing is 'natural' in any way. It has to be learnt painstakingly over a period of several years.

The notion that writing is in essence a record of

speech through a set of widely-accepted graphemes, is open to question, despite the apparent validity of the notion. Some kinds of writing in the far-east represent the semantic content of language rather than its sounds, others in most parts of Asia and the west represent the phonemic content of language. The second kind, to which the writing systems of English and Urdu belong, employs loose, inadequate representations of the sounds of the languages involved. A limited number of conventional symbols are used singly or in combination with others to indicate sounds, individually and collectively, but it is clear that it is a makeshift affair.

Forty four sounds are said to exist in the Received Pronunciation of British English, for which an alphabet of 26 letters is used. In fact, if the allophones are added, the number of sounds is greater; if, further, one were to talk about the subtle vocal signals that enable a listener to determine the difference between, say, ' a maze' and 'amaze' or 'may be' and 'maybe,' the number grows yet further to perhaps a hundred or more sounds. Likewise, the alphabet contains no provision for the large semantic content of gesture, stress and intonation, factors crucial to the understanding of oral language. A punctuation system has evolved over the centuries to indicate, very inappropriately, some of these factors, (obviously nothing can be done about gesture and very little can be done about intonation), but it is not fully stable even today. Its representation of suprasegmentals is imperfect at best-- and whimsical, subjective or even quite damaging to the decoding process of writing at worst.

It is suggested that writing is, therefore, intrinsically different from speaking. There is some truth in the observation that 'literacy' involves a second learning in a different medium of the same language, and that, while it has obvious links, it is not merely an extension of the first one. An 'orate' man has learnt his language *once,* in a natural setting. A 'literate' man has learnt it *twice,* the second time in a different and relatively unnatural context. It is not surprising, therefore, to find many people who function painlessly in an aural/oral atmosphere and who might be able to read quite well, but who are hesitant about writing, even in the mother-tongue. The difficulties are aggravated when it is not the mother-tongue. Being orate and literate in *two* languages means that a person has used his innate language learning mechanisms *four times,* in various settings, both natural and artificial; a heavy linguistic burden indeed.

However, in fairness to the argument, it has been suggested that there is no significantly qualitative difference between the skills of oracy and literacy, and that in literate societies they can proceed together fairly naturally *if a child is introduced to them early enough.* Loban found that advantages gained at the beginning of school were retained at the end of it, and that bright beginners were bright enders, suggesting that an infant's innate language ability had something to do with the acquisition of effective reading and writing skills. A child's exposure to all aspects of language would probably begin very early, within months of its birth, in a literate, media rich society such as that of America. Almost any child there would be subjected to, nay saturated by, a pervasive, sustained commercial onslaught, both spoken and written.

Krashen *(The Role of Input (reading) and Instruction*

in Developing Writing Ability, a paper presented at the University of Southern California, 1981) indicates a link between reading and writing, suggesting that a good reader will probably be a good writer as well. He asserts that 'all good writers will have done large amounts of pleasure reading.'(9)

Now, reverting for a moment to the skills of listening and speaking, while the link is incontrovertible, especially when one considers the deaf child who remains dumb because he cannot hear what people around him are saying, even these two skills might remain developmentally unequal in 'normal' children; ('normality' is difficult to describe in the endlessly complex emotional and intellectual dynamics of human relationships). An individual might understand another person without effort (be a good listener), but might be reluctant to offer anything himself (be a poor speaker). *Competence* exceeds *performance* in such cases, and the disparity might be exacerbated by a host of factors. Natural mental laziness, shyness, overbearing siblings or parents, social status or hypercritical, insensitive teachers—any one, or some, or all of these together, might severely inhibit his natural desire to communicate.

The researcher has not come across any commentary that suggests that there is no link between the skills. The link between listening and speaking is too obvious to be ignored, but it must be stated that at some stage the skills can continue separately. A person grown stone deaf is still able to speak. So also, though writing and reading mean a great deal to each other in the beginning, it is possible for a person to continue to write, though perhaps not as efficiently as before, long after his fading eyesight has made it difficult or impossible for him to read. The indispensable part of the linkage is when the contingent productive skills are being formed from the base receptive skills; (there may be some mutual formation here; the productive skills probably help the receptive ones as well, i.e., writing might help reading); but they can develop a life of their own.

The link between reading and writing is less evident than the link between listening and speaking. It is possible to find good writers who are not especially fond of reading. According to Ben Jonson Shakespeare was not a particularly well-read man, though we should measure this observation relatively, against Jonson's own impressive standards of scholarship. The University Wits were probably greater readers than Shakespeare, yet who among them could compare with him in writing? Is one to assume that some, or indeed many, components of Shakespeare's considerable range of knowledge were acquired from sources other than direct reading? If he had picked up his knowledge from discussions with others he must have had a retentive memory for the spoken word. However, all this is possible. One has it on Jane Austen's admission that she was no great scholar, yet hardly anybody in the nineteenth century can compare with her in writing. Jack London was more a man of action than a scholar, yet he was an effective writer.

Some researchers question whether the link is significant, weakening the apparently obvious but possibly naive assumption that these two skills go together (10). At the University of Southern California, Irene Clark (mentioned in reference 10) found no significant correlation between writing ability and reading background. Most people associated with academics, teachers and students alike, claim to be avid readers--and, of course, many are. However, very few of these self-confessed omniverous readers are good at writing. Even if some correlation is found, it is difficult to infer a *causal* relationship, namely, that sustained reading *results in* superior writing.

Some good writers happen to be big readers. Some big readers can write quite well when they try. Some big readers are terrible writers. One must assume that good writers are good writers for some reason other than reading.

Notice has to be taken of non- linguistic factors like diffidence or laziness. They certainly affect linguistic performance. Children whose personalities are crushed by dictatorial parents or who are ridiculed by heedless peers or siblings might become hesitant about language. They will find it easier to sink into the receptive mode than to make an effort to enter the productive one. The receptive skills are easier than the productive skills and, of the productive skills, speaking is easier than writing. It is more comfortable to listen than to speak, and much more comfortable to listen, read or speak than to write. Somebody else does the hard work of thinking, speaking and writing.

The receptive attitude to language is reinforced by the college lecturing system. A few teachers drone on and on while many students listen, sometimes for hours on end. The dulling effect can be imagined: but even more dangerous is the inculcation of passive communicational habits. Interruption or participation is discouraged in what is essentially an authoritative system. In the interests of administration and good classroom management, especially when there are huge classes, some sort of discipline is required. But one result of this is that while South Asian students might hesitantly offer a little when they are asked to speak, they will offer hardly anything when they are asked to write.

The motor aspects should not be ignored, either. Writers who get cramps sometimes notice that the flow of ideas seems to suffer because the muscles of their hands are not working properly, pointing to a reverse causal link between the physical and the intellectual. Speakers suffering from sore throats might notice something similar. It might be going too far to suggest that one can write basically because one's hands are trained to do so, or that one finds ideas to speak because the speech organs are functioning properly, suggesting thereby that thinking follows physical conditioning. One's intuition rejects such a hypothesis, but not entirely. Despite the apparent concurrency of events physical and mental, primacy must go to the brain in these matters. Research by Benjamin Libet indicates that unconscious mental activity can precede consciousness by as much as a third of a second--which means that the decision to write, the several decisions about *what* to write and the numerous decisions attendant upon *how* to write it, all come before the awareness of those decisions. This would suggest that conscious decision-making is impossible—we do not look at alternatives consciously and then make informed decisions about them. Unknown activities go on in our unconscious minds. These activities make decisions for us, and only then, perhaps a third of second later, do we become aware of them. However, the physical probably can, and does, affect the mental.

The premise behind these comments is that while writing is crucial to academic performance, it is the skill that receives the least conscious attention in the Pakistani educational set up. Teachers seem to think that this skill will take care of itself. Too many students suffer, not because they are unintelligent or lack ideas, but because they are poor at expressing themselves in writing in the second language. There is hardly any need to repeat the truism that ninety-nine per cent of the time a student is judged by what he writes.

Language is not only an academic activity, it is also a social one, something which is done between people for overt or covert reasons. Writing is the least natural, but academically the most important, of the skills. The foregoing arguments have been presented to raise the question as to whether the skills are fully or partly separable, or whether they should be taken together. How much can one talk about teaching a writing course isolated from speaking, listening or reading? Is it better to keep the skills separate, or to employ them together in an integrated teaching mode? Every inter-activity uses language to some degree, be it jotting down a quick memo, asking the family what to cook for lunch, or instructing one's son to tie up the buffalo for the night.

How much writing competence is required for any given society or segment of society is arguable. For rural areas probably not very much; a few scribes can serve a whole community, as most of the essential information will be passed around by word of mouth. For an industrialised, urbanised society a wide-spread working level of writing competence is predicated. As a society develops and becomes more intricate and more dependent on technology and on the storage and retrieval of knowledge, the skills of reading and writing assume a central position for both national and individual fulfillment. And for students at the graduate and post-graduate levels, regardless of whether their background is rural or urban, regardless of whether or not they achieve their ends in life, there is no question but that a high degree of writing competence is indispensable.

The history of Pakistan illustrates, or at least indicates, this assertion. Different figures are mentioned by different agencies, but literacy has probably grown from less than 20 per cent to something near 50 per cent over the last half century, indicating a movement away from the country's agrarian underpinnings towards greater urbanisation and industrialisation. The definition of literacy in South Asia is somewhat like that in the nineteenth century for rural America, namely, little more than an ability to scratch out a few names in some language. But this does indicate a growing awareness of the advantages of literacy. Being able to keep records or write letters to one's associates is a big step forward in corporate living. Being able to pick through newspapers and magazines for relevant information would undoubtedly help in many aspects of modern living, from modernising agricultural procedures to keeping abreast with the news. There are those who argue that the rise of the electronic culture means the downfall of the written word, and that people are returning to the oral culture of their forebears. For example, one student claimed that his computer would 'correct' his outpourings, so there was no need for him to strain his mind over obsolete trivialities like spelling and punctuation.

A teacher has to contend with such attitudes. There is as yet little evidence to support the assertion that writing skills have become or are becoming obsolete. Good, clear writing in English is required as never before, especially in the global village. It is required for international trade, for aviation, for understanding new kinds of technology, for acquiring information about all sorts of things, for diplomacy and for the dissemination of knowledge. The electronic voice-mail might supersede the electronic e-mail in the computer world, but only for limited social interchange. Books cost much less than these gadgets. They pack a lot into a small space, are light and readily transportable and do not depend on the availability of electricity. When a visual medium is required to reinforce and fix the spoken word, it moves inevitably back to the written word. Writing is still, and will remain for the foreseeable future, the primary repository of knowledge. The functioning of the computer itself depends very heavily on writing. But, at the same time, we have to admit that the computer is developing its own methods and conventions, and that these might affect traditional forms of written communication. It might even affect spelling and structure with sufficient consistency to change the language. Technology can have a strong blowback effect. For example, e-mail has supplanted letter writing for many people, and it is rapidly developing its own conventions in abbreviations and idiom.

Teaching Approaches

Two approaches to teaching writing are identified. The first focuses on the end product, the second on the components of the activity. The 'product' approach is the older one and still has almost universal currency in Pakistan. A topic is given, perhaps a little preliminary discussion is done in class, perhaps a model is supplied, and the student then struggles to compose an essay on it. Spelling, punctuation, idiom and grammar are then 'corrected' by the teacher in marginal notes, and, if the class is small enough, some verbal feedback is given. The hope is that the student will not repeat his mistakes in future assignments. The sad fact is that he *will* do so, much to the disappointment or fury of the teacher, who might begin to think that he is dealing with morons.

Focusing on the end rather than on the means has another undesirable effect. Since the product is what earns students either praise or castigation, and since most people prefer to be praised, they look for ready-made answers and copy them out or learn them by heart for their tests. Teachers and examiners then get pieces worthy of a Macaulay of which not a word is the student's own. This practice is now widespread in Pakistan.

It is said that one learns even by cheating. One would not mind if at the end of it the students acquired some of the linguistic facility of the pieces they copy, but this is not evident when they are called upon to write something unaided. The lack of transference is especially obvious in extended assignments where well-worded passages lifted unacknowledged from elsewhere are mixed with atrocious ones all too obviously written by the student.

Exposing students to models of good writing is a method that has come down from antiquity. The pedagogical expectation is that the students will imbibe something of the sample's excellence. They are told to emulate that kind of writing, but are cautioned that emulation does not mean the same as copying. Students are then faced with the conundrum of being both similar and different at the same time. If they choose the same topic, there seems little point in trying to change or improve something which is obviously very appropriate for that topic. Any change seems a change for the worse. If they choose another topic, they might find it difficult to write in the style adopted by the model author for his topic. Style is not something general, that is, something universal in approach and usage suitable for all topics; it is best when it is seen to be appropriate for the specific topic in hand. Few students manage to produce anything worthwhile. In this author's experience, this method does not achieve much.

Alternatively, they are asked to make original critical estimations of pieces of good writing. This is done in all literature courses from high school upwards. It is like asking a poor man to offer alms to a rich man. The hope is that the attempt to analyse a good writer's thoughts and language will give a student some insights into worthwhile ideas and good language, and that these insights will filter through to his own writing. This rarely happens.

It seems strange that copying out, or learning tracts of good English by heart, or analyzing literary pieces, should not result in an ability to write good English, but there it is. It arises from an old notion that language consists of learning so many correct utterances, whereas it is really a complex system that enables one to generate appropriate utterances. The background to this will be discussed later.

Recent classroom practice focuses more on the means than on the end. Some questioning of the effectiveness of the 'end product' approach took place in the sixties and seventies. What we have now is a step forward in teaching writing. As Williams says:

> '.... work over the last fifteen years suggests that teaching writing effectively has two crucial elements: that we provide students with situations where language can be used meaningfully, and that we focus attention on and emphasize the act of writing itself, not finished essays.'(11)

The new recommendation emphasises stages in the activity:

> 'Effective writing instruction, it was argued, would focus on helping students through these various stages. To achieve this aim, classrooms were to become 'writing workshops' where students shared their work with one another and where the teacher intervened regularly as compositions were developed through several drafts. The emphasis was on process rather than product. This approach to composition instruction, kown as the 'process view,' has supplanted the product view in most of the nation's universities, and in a large percentage of its school districts.'(12)

The nation mentioned here is America. Of special interest to this writer is the statement that the process approach was applied at the *university* level. The university teacher normally gets the end product of years of low motivation and unimaginative, stereotyped learning and teaching approaches, when bad habits are so deeply etched in the language mechanisms of his students, that there seems little hope of erasing them. There is never enough time in these days of overflowing classrooms and packed syllabuses to help students unlearn old habits and encourage new ones in their place.

Nevertheless, the effort should be made. This writer is admittedly, and very humbly, rather less enamoured of right 'methods' than some of the writers cited here. There is probably no magical, hidden button, known to only a few people which, once discovered and pressed in the proper way, makes everything fall in place. There are probably no short-cuts in the long, hard haul of language learning.

Excessive concentration on means rather than on ends might also be self-defeating, as something has to be left for resolution by the student's own cognitive, synthesising faculties. He cannot be led by the hand at every stage. More, he *ought not* to be led so, especially if he is already a young adult. A certain degree of autonomy and personal control should be fostered.

However, anything that might facilitate the skills of writing, either in the beginning of the learning process, or in between, or somewhere near the end of a student's academic life (the main concern of this work), should be tested. There is a consistent and pervasive writing problem among senior students in Pakistan. One should do what one can to ameliorate it.

Grammar

The author cannot speak for other South Asian countries, though looking at some writings emanating from them he would probably not be far wrong in suggesting that conditions there are much the same. The teaching of grammar in Pakistan appears to have learnt little from developments abroad. Old Latinate moulds and paradigms still dominate, and there is a deficient appreciation of the fact of change in language. An obsession with 'correct' and 'incorrect' stipulations prevails today in much the same way as it did forty years ago. As far as this researcher can see, one reason for this is that linguistics has not really gained a foothold in these areas. Planners, teachers and administrators are not aware of these developments, or, if they are, are not impressed by them.

Two important developments in the approach to grammar in the twentieth century are outlined here. The first challenged the prescriptive, punitive, rule-giving concept of grammar which is still in vogue in South Asia, and suggested that the true purpose of grammar was to describe the language as it was actually used. The second proposed a dynamic, generative model which accounted for some aspects of language that had hitherto proved puzzling.

Historically, Ben Jonson's *English Grammar* (1640) might be the first attempt to understand English without reference to Latin models. Nevertheless, later grammarians continued with the 'corrective' approach, and Latin was taught as the prime model of linguistic accuracy upon which English structure was supposed to be based. An educated Englishman might even write in Latin, in preference to his own language. Bacon's *Novum Organum* (1620) illustrates this point, although more than almost any other writer one can think of at that time, he developed models in good prose for his own language. Even a writer as good as Dryden could be somewhat contemptuous of English as a language, and could assert that it had no workable grammar of its own.

About two hundred and fifty Latinised English grammar books were produced in the eighteenth century alone. This, of course, was the 'Augustan' age, which aligned itself with the ideals and cultural assumptions of the Latin world in Rome under the Emperor Augustus. The Latin perception lingered well into the next century. Originally a 'grammar' school was a school where Latin grammar rather than English grammar was taught. Such schools catered to members of a large and increasingly prosperous middle class seeking to better their social standing. Precision and grace in language were pre-requisites in the pursuit of this ambition, and it was asserted that touchstones for these qualities could come only from Latin.

In the eighteenth century came writers such as Sheridan who (quoting an unnamed prelate) mourned the mistakes of some of the most celebrated writers of English (13) *[General Dictionary of the English Language,* 1780]; or Cobbett, who complained that Milton made errors in great number; or Swift, who called for an English academy on the lines of the French and Spanish ones to halt the disturbing process of 'decay' in the language. Quaint as such statements might now appear, they foreshadow some attitudes encountered in academic circles in Pakistan today.

In general, the approach in the seventeenth and eighteenth centuries was that language was divinely inspired, and was, therefore, perfect and immutable (all deviations were for the worse and were the result of human wickedness), that Latin had preserved linguistic perfection more than other languages, and that English could be saved from decay or improved by fitting it into the Latin mould. Southey made fun of this approach by stating that Latin must be the first of all languages, because the call of sea birds was 'qua-a-qua', and 'aqua' is the Latin word for water. Such attitudes lead us to recall, also, the experiments with two children shut off from all human interaction mounted by Psammeticos, a seventh-century B.C. Egyptian king. He is said to have observed that the first word spoken by those children was 'bekos,' the Phrygian word for bread, and concluded that Phrygian was therefore the very first of all human languages. Of course, much could be found wrong with the experiment, as also with his inferences and conclusions, but which brave person in those tyrannical times would dare to question the king? Which brave person in modern tyrannical times would dare to question the ruler, temporary or permanent? Very little has changed over the centuries.

However, some changes can be observed. It was not until the end of the nineteenth century that a few people began to question the Latin premise. Historical linguists such as Jespersen *(The Outline and Structure of English,* 1894, and *The Philosophy of Grammar,* 1924) pointed out the phenomenon of change and heretically suggested that change did not corrupt a language. Linguists nowadays take much for granted which would have been incomprehensible to grammarians in the eighteenth and nineteenth centuries. "Corrective' grammar, which derives its authority from another language (exonormative) or from definitive expositions of its own grammar, has been replaced by 'helpful' grammar which derives its authority from actual usage within the language itself (endonormative).

In part, the new perception resulted from the observations of people like Boas and Bloomfield following their attempts to understand and analyse some American Indian languages. It was discovered that traditional grammar was inadequate for the purpose, forcing the early commentators into a new mould of thinking. 'Phrase structure' grammar, as this kind of descriptive grammar was called, took as its starting point the scientific description of language. The effects of this are still here. Grammar no longer leads, it follows, and when it observes alteration in the thing it follows, it changes itself accordingly.

However, side by side with these developments came the counterattacks of the prescriptionists. The preferred word now was 'usage' rather than 'rule', but this made little difference to the approach. A few well-known names are mentioned here: Fowler's *Modern English Usage* (Oxford, 1934;-a hint that one's own English might be old-fashioned), Partridge's *Usage and Abusage* (Penguin, 1963:- a warning that there was such a thing as 'abusage'), Vallins' series, *Good English, Better English* and *The Best English* (Pan, different dates:- an assertion that there were degrees of 'goodness' in language) among others--the list of such books is long. The projection of 'correct' and 'incorrect' values with regard to language has taken a long time to subside in the west, and the subsidence is not complete by any means. It is still very much in evidence in Pakistan.

The second big development in grammar is the idea of language as a flexible, generative system rather than a collection of 'right' expressions (14). The permutations and combinations of the vertical elements in the vocabulary (or vocabularies) of a language, with the horizontal elements in its structure or inner organisation, enable a speaker to generate in theory an infinite number of acceptable utterances. In fact, there are physical and mental limits to what he can produce. However, if just one example is taken, 'John drives a car', and if 'John' is replaced in turn with the names of all people in the world with different names, a few billion utterances will have been produced; and if pronouns are substituted for nouns, a good few more again. All this is possible with the subject noun alone. If other parts of the sentence are replaced or twisted around to a passive construction, or pluralized, or taken into different tenses, or changed to the negative or interrogative, the possibilities become astronomical. The point is that by playing about with the elements of a simple sentence within a general understanding of the structure of a given language, one can go on and on spinning new and perfectly acceptable utterances.

Since some aspects (not all) of what is now called transformational-generative grammar (T-G grammar) are relevant to this study it will be discussed in greater detail later. Among the models available so far, this one offers insights which might prove useful. It does not lay down the law as in traditional grammar. It does not simply describe a language as in descriptive grammar. It goes further than both in attempting to explain how the language works as well. If traditional grammar is deductive and descriptive grammar inductive, then generative grammar is explorative. However, the presentation of T-G grammar has suffered from some of the prime-mover's personal interests. The existence of kernel structures and the 'rules' whereby they are transformed, to surface structures can only be assumed; nothing here can be tested, measured or established. And Chomsky wanted to make it seem all mathematical and scientific, so the net outcome is unhelpful as it stands, at least for classroom teaching. Some rough logic is visible in human language, but there is also a lot that defies logic. And how, for example, would those 'inverted tree' diagrams help in clarifying a rudimentary utterance in English? For one, those hanging trees do not reflect one's internal image of the language. For another, how would one set about explaining the formation of such diagrams to students still struggling with the bare beginnings of the second language in a selection of words that makes sense to them? And, having learnt the formation of such diagrams, would they become better at generating acceptable utterances in English? One has one's doubts.

Ground realities in Pakistan must be taken into consideration. There is only one criterion for the acceptance or rejection of a new theory or pedagogical recommendation; how useful is it likely to be for second language learners in this country? The author's reaction is that such diagrams waste time. They also muddy that which is already murky. They might give pleasure to pedants with a mathematical bent of mind, but in adding yet another layer of barely relevant learning to the already difficult task of writing in the second language, they do very little for the student. Here it might be mentioned that most generative grammarians feel that speech and writing are distinct linguistic conventions of the same language and that each has its own way of tackling the business of communication. In English we find some areas where the *grammar* of the two conventions differ, such as the oral device of showing parts of speech by stress in certain words, which cannot be shown in writing. Only one example will be given here—the word 'import' whether noun or a verb looks the same when it is written, but in spoken English the first part of the word is stressed for the noun and the second for the verb. Some of these considerations will be taken up later.

A lot of time is spent at school learning traditional grammar. Apart from the sheer tedium of the exercise, most of it goes over the children's heads. But traditional grammar is popular with teachers, first because they are familiar with it, and second because they think they know what to do with it. There are rules (whether valid or not is not their concern). There are exercises and drills. Something seems to get across, even if the students are bored and restless. After all, some of them eventually get the trick of filling in blanks and putting in correct forms of verbs, so there is a sense of satisfaction at the end of the session.

The shock comes when they are asked to produce the language themselves. All that rule giving and correcting and drilling does not seem to lead to a generalised ability to generate acceptable utterances in the language, and this deficiency is carried over from year to year. If the end of grammar teaching is to produce students who can use the language in different situations in speaking and writing, this end is rarely achieved. One must question the validity of the approach. The occasional student will rise above the system on mysterious merits of his own. The vast majority will come out of it with inadequate acquisitions and faulty perspectives.

Yet Pakistani teachers persist. Grammar is part of the mythology of language teaching. Planners and teachers are reluctant either to change or to let go of it. There is a vague feeling that it is central to the whole process. The usual justifications are (1) that it sharpens and disciplines the mind, or (2) that it helps one to understand how a language works, or (3) that it makes it easier for the student when he sets out to learn another language, or (4) that it makes one a better reader, writer or interpreter of literature.

Probably none of these justifications would stand an empirical test. As early as 1906 (see F. Hoyt in *Teachers College Record*, November 1906) one researcher discovered that grammar fed in large quantities to immature children tended to retard rather than facilitate their natural development. The second justification might have some validity, but knowing the theory of swimming will not usually make a person a good swimmer. The third justification might or might not be valid. The grammar of one language cannot be imposed on another without damaging it, but it might make access to that language somewhat easier, especially in the beginning. And there seems to be almost no link between the study of grammar and the appreciation of literature.

This is how the *Encyclopedia of Educational Research* (1950) (15) summarised it:

> *[On disciplining the mind]:* experimentation in this area failed to yield any significant evidence supporting the belief in grammar as a disciplinary subject.

> *[On the interpretation of literature]:* results from tests in grammar, composition, and literary interpretation led to the conclusion that there was little or no relationship between grammar and composition and grammar and literary interpretation.

> *[On improved writing and usage]:* further evidence supplementing the early studies indicated that training in formal grammar did not transfer to any significant extent to writing or to recognising correct English. In general the experimental evidence revealed a discouraging lack of relationship between grammatical knowledge and the better utilisation of expressional skills. Recently, grammar has been held to contribute to the better understanding of the sentence. Yet even here, *there is a discouraging lack of relationship between sentence sense and grammatical knowledge of subjects and predicates.* (author's emphasis)

[On the study of foreign languages]: in spite of the fact that the contribution of the knowledge of English grammar to achievement in foreign languages has been its chief justification in the past, the experimental evidence does not support this conclusion.

[On the improvement of reading]: the study of grammar has been justified because of its possible contribution to reading skills, but the evidence does not support this conclusion.

[On improved language behaviour in general]: no more relationship exists between knowledge of grammar and the application of the knowledge in a functional language situation than exists between any two different and unrelated subjects.

[On diagramming sentences]: the use of sentence diagramming as a method of developing sentence mastery and control over certain mechanical skills closely related to the sentence has been subjected to a series of experimental investigations. In general the studies indicate that diagramming is a skill which, while responsive to instruction, has very slight value in itself. There is no point in training the pupil to diagram sentences except for the improvement it brings in his ability to create effective sentences. The evidence shows that this is insignificant.

These comments are well over half a century old. In essence what they imply is that learning the rules of grammar means learning the rules of grammar, not how to use the language; and that learning how to make sentence diagrams means learning how to make sentence diagrams, not how to use the language. They confirm the tenuous relationship between the formal study of grammar and usable language skills. It is akin to expecting a man to get into an aeroplane and pilot it around the airfield just because he has undergone an exacting course in aerodynamics, and then wondering what went wrong when he crashed into a tree on take off.

Yet grammar is still seen as the central prop in the language teaching complex, and conservative educators are reluctant to abandon it. What concerns language teachers is the relationship between grammar and writing. Traditionally, the two have been closely associated throughout history. In fact, the primary connotation of the original Greek word for grammar is writing. It has acquired a separate crust of meaning through the centuries, and now generally denotes a body of rules to govern, or in more recent years, to describe, or yet more recently, to explain, the organic working of a language.

It is of interest to try and understand the reasons for this reluctance to abandon grammar. The primary reason in Pakistan is the deficient language of teachers themselves, especially at the middle school level. It is possible to teach the grammar of a language without really knowing the language itself, since all or most of the explaining is done in a Pakistani regional language. For such people, teaching the grammar of the English language is easier than teaching the English language.

The second big reason is that traditional grammar gives firm rules and recommendations, making it easier for the teacher to state, evaluate or defend different aspects of the language.

Other apparently valid reasons exist, usually in higher classes. This author has encountered a certain level of cynicism among educators about so-called scientific studies, because too often the findings of one study are contradicted a few months or years later by those of another. This can happen because the groups tested are not truly representative or truly appropriate for the purposes of the study, or because the playing field is not, in fact cannot be, truly level. It can happen because circumstances change, which means that the findings of such-and-such study might be valid for that study conducted at that time and under those conditions alone, but that extrapolations to the world at large are suspect. Compensatory and self-validating mechanisms are built into the procedures under which these studies are conducted, but at best they point to trends or approximations, at worst they can lead to downright misrepresentations. The controls are not infallible, nor is it possible to put complex human beings into neat compartments. The conservative approach towards grammar finds other justifications for itself. What seems true for odd groups of students in Britain or America might not be true for Pakistani students. Perhaps these studies are right. Perhaps they are wrong. If right, Pakistani students will indeed have wasted some time. If wrong, a whole generation of students will have been put at risk.

Writing

Some interesting experiments have taken place in the ongoing search for ways to improve the teaching of reading and writing. One recalls efforts in Britain some decades ago to introduce young children to a modified phonetic spelling called the Initial Teaching Alphabet (developed by Sir James Pitman), a spelling system which attempted to preserve the 'whole' appearance of a word without being obsessed by 'rightness' as defined in orthodox spelling. This was in deference to Gestalt theory in the first quarter of the twentieth century, namely, that the brain tends to perceive wholes, or *gestalts,* before it moves to an examination of parts.

The brave but perhaps unsupportable prediction that children would pass painlessly to orthodox alphabetic spelling in the fullness of time (two or three years) was not consistently realised, and there was a subsequent outcry among university teachers that the school system was producing illiterates.

The enthusiasm for change is laudable. However, what seems like impeccable theory might not always stand up to scrutiny, and what seems workable under controlled conditions might not be so in the real world, although die-hards will insist that the scrutiny rather than the theory is at fault. Research, field-study, long-term experimentation and large measures of scepticism are required at every stage in the process.

At the same time too much scepticism can lead to paralysis. The Pakistani system tends to follow western conservatism in this regard. Educational planners usually have a 'let's wait and see' attitude to things, especially when radical theories are propounded. They tend to kill healthy movements before they can take hold in the classroom. If they take hold, as in the experiment outlined previously, they are killed by accusations that standards are being lowered. This happened to the recommendations of people like Thorndike and Dewey in the early part of the twentieth century and later to the works of Smith and Goodman. The system does not bend itself to changing needs or educational developments, despite its visible imperfections and the fact that it cannot seem to attain its own objectives. At no time can it be said to have functioned in an efficient, humane or rational way.

Of interest to writing teachers is what the foregoing experiment claimed to have achieved: the release of a flood of writing energy because children were no longer terrorised into immobility by the 'correct/incorrect' sword hanging over their heads. *Whatever* they wrote was acceptable as a record of their ideas, provided the spelling was reasonably representative of the words they used. Thus liberated from the shackles of an insistently perfectionist approach, they wrote freely.

If one can help students to overcome their lack of confidence and get them to write, a big step forward will have been made. There is a persistent spelling problem in Pakistan also, but the real problem is with grammar. School *beginners* in Britain would certainly know the base structures of their own language well before the age of six. It cannot be assumed that school *enders* in Pakistan, even at the ages of sixteen or seventeen, have mastered those structures. In addition to spelling, to release any kind of writing energy in English in this country, one would have to liberate students from the paralysis of the 'correct/incorrect' approach to teaching grammar.

Right or wrong, the study of grammar as the basis either of second language learning, or as a method of improving the use of the first language, has a hoary antiquity to it. More will have to be said about grammar later. At the moment, teachers are caught between the rigidity of traditional grammar, the flexibility of descriptive grammar, and the complexity of T-G grammar. In terms of what satisfies second language students (even if the way it does it is unsatisfactory), the first kind still scores highest. Flexibility and 'chaos' theories are all very well, but students want to know precisely what should or should not be done. They are not interested in different expressions and dialects. And the more modern terminological baggage of determiners, modifiers, continuants, adjuncts, disjuncts, etc., not to mention those incomprehensible charts and diagrams, seems to clarify little. Traditional 'this-is-right/that-is-wrong' grammar still holds sway.

At this stage it should be enough for the researcher to state his own position in the debate, namely, that grammar is useful, but that it should be taught with the end purpose of language facility in mind, and should not become an end in itself. Nor should it be tested as a separate entity. If a student can produce acceptable utterances, his internalised knowledge of the language will be tested anyhow. If he makes mistakes, there might be more effective ways of correcting them than sending him back to grammatical rules. The question is not a settled one. The language teacher struggles with the imperfections of language in general, and tries his best.

Linguists have challenged the old teaching assumptions about grammar. They have suggested new ways of looking at grammar and language. But they have not really given the teacher a replacement for the tools he had before. Until they can do so definitively, the old blunt, inappropriate tools will have to be kept in circulation, except that now there is little excuse for using them in the old, ineffective ways.

Writing, like all manifestations of language, is a complicated activity. In subsequent chapters, some attempt will be made to analyse what goes on in the mind of a person when he writes, and to suggest at which points a teacher can help in the process. Pakistani students continue to be diffident about writing. The 'correct/incorrect' approach leaves lasting strains on their linguistic confidence. While they might be willing to engage in conversation because of its evanescence, their writing is open to scrutiny by many critical eyes, and there is no escape.

S.I Hayakawa said the following a long time ago. It strikes this author as relevant to Pakistani students trying to use English for advanced studies today:

> '...the most common result of the teaching of English and composition is not the creation of good writers and speakers, but the creation, in most of the public, of a lifelong fear of grammatical errors...to be sure, we help some of our students to speak and write better. But the majority of fair-to-middling students leave the class feeling that 'correct English', like moral perfection, is something that they

cannot hope to attain. Burdened, as the result of our castigations, by a sense of linguistic Original Sin, they depart from school feeling, like those Puritans who felt that whatever was fun must be sinful, that whatever sounds natural must be wrong. It is tragic that most Americans suffer, with respect to the use of their own language, especially in formal or semi-formal situations, a discomfort or malaise that can only be described as a mild form of neurosis... '(16)

Hayakawa is an American talking about Americans, about people using *their own* language. The concern here is young Pakistanis petrified by the seemingly endless traps of a *second* language.

Hayakawa goes on to give an example:

'...I vividly remember a student of mine, an elementary school teacher, who, when asked to write a theme in class, went into a more than acute anxiety state. In the course of the first 50 minutes, she wore four or five holes in her sheet of paper with repeated erasures; she chewed an eight inch pencil down to two inches: she displayed the classic psychosomatic symptoms of anxiety, trembling, flushing and sweating...'(17)

Hayakawa observed this 'writing anxiety' in an American *teacher*, not a student. All teachers of writing will have similar stories to tell. The present author has had reactions ranging from hysteria and attempts to hide the answer sheets on one side, to sullen resentment and flat refusals to cooperate on the other. Asking a student to write is the moment of truth for him. It is like forcing him to display what he thinks is his grammatical uncertainty, something he is otherwise able most of the time to conceal fairly well in the give-and-take of rapid conversation helped along in this country with a large measure of random switching between two or three languages.

Hayakawa has the final word here as well:

> 'We have all experienced, too, the embarrassed silence that occurs among many social groups when they find that an English teacher is in their midst...I mention these familiar experiences in order to underline the fact that, in linguistic as in other behaviour, when people do not know how to act and cannot figure out how to discover how to act, and when previous attempts to act appropriately have repeatedly been met with failure or censure, the result cannot but be some kind of anxiety state...just as the old-fashioned , two-valued morality of Absolute Evil was charged by Dr. Oliver Wendell Holmes to be a contributory cause of mental illness, so does it now appear that the old-fashioned, two-valued grammar of 'correct' versus 'incorrect' English is a contributory cause of the more or less grave linguistic neuroses that most people suffer from... '(18)

Working forward from this, if this is true about

Americans using their own language, how much truer must it be for Pakistanis using a language that is not their own? Teachers in this country, of course, do not really need further confirmation of something they encounter every day. Pakistanis in general hate the chore of writing in English, no matter how facile they might be when they speak the language, as many are. In a few one gets the robust counter-reaction of, 'well, it's not my language; it's not fair to expect perfection. I'll write it as I think I should, and there's an end to it.' Surprisingly, such people tend to be more productive than those who worry about the correctness of every word before they put it down on paper.

If not the correction of incorrect formulations, what, then, are teachers of English to do? Teachers are habituated to correcting scripts. How else are they to instruct their students in proper writing usage? Between the old-type teacher who has studied traditional grammar but knows nothing about linguistics, and the more modern teacher who does, correcting or permitting usage in language is still the most common way of things. The modem teacher will be slightly less rigid and will accept constructions like, 'it's me', or, 'everyone ate their food', because descriptive grammar tells him that this is how most native speakers actually use these expressions (not, 'it is *I*', or, 'everyone ate *his* food', which is how the old prescriptions would have it).

In fact the modem teacher, like his conservative colleague, misses the point. It is not validating and invalidating constructions that matter very much, though they have their place. What really matters is a comprehension of the dynamics of the language.

There is another kind of teacher who uses the linguistic approach. This is the one who understands that, while there is a common platform in the dialects that form a language, the variations are almost endless; that since a language keeps on changing, its rules cannot be immutable; that language is a kind of behaviour; that the goodness or badness of language should be judged by external factors, since there is nothing *intrinsically* good or bad about any utterance; and that the teacher's primary role is to help his students observe how the language works.

In summary, when one sees so many students entering graduate courses who cannot write English, one must question attitudes and approaches current in this country with regard to the teaching and learning of this most important skill of this most important world language. Since 1974, this author has participated as supervisor, resource person or observer in several workshops to upgrade teacher skills, and to suggest ways of improving conditions in ELT. These are the ones he knows about. Innumerable other similar workshops have been held all round the country, of which he has no direct knowledge. A quarter of a century later, he can see no improvement.

Many causes for this failure can be cited. However, the primary blame, as far as the author can see, is the delay in starting English until a child is eleven or twelve years old, long after his extraordinary aptitude for learning languages has faded. Languages can certainly be learnt after the age of six or seven, or even thirteen or fourteen, but the effort to do so is progressively greater, and the results are less certain.

The school syllabus pattern was decided many years

ago for the main educational system in the country in accordance with the theory available at that time. That theory is outdated. In any case, no curricular decision should be left untested for decades. Four years is long enough to see if something is working or not. The curriculum should not have hardened into an irreversible pattern. English should be taught from the beginning.

Chapter 2 Notes

1. Clark, H., and Clark, E., *Psychology and Language,* Harcourt Brace Jovanovich, NY, 1977,298

2. Bryson, B., *Mother-Tongue; the English Language,* Penguin, 1990, 7. Bryson has no doubts about this: "...indeed, children in the first five years have such a remarkable facility for language that they can effortlesly learn two structurally different languages simultaneously..."

3. Chomsky, N., *Language and Mind,* Harcourt Brace Jovanovich, NY, 46 and passim

4. Lender, C, 'Early Childhood Development from Two to Six Years of Age", Internct, 1999

5. For example, the loss of the 'thee/thou' forms with their attendant inflections. Also, the change in 'question-asking' structures

6. Aitcheson, J., *The Articulate Mammal,* Routledge, London and NY, 1995,20

7. Krashen, S., *Writing research, Theory and Applications,* Pergamon, NY, 23, 1987

8. Lender, Ibid

9. Loban, W., in Williams, D., *Preparing to Teach Writing,* Lawrence Erlbaum,NJ, 1996,63-64

10. Williams, Ibid., 3

11. Ibid., 64

12. Ibid., 7

13. Ibid., 8

14. In Postman, N., and Weingartner, C, *Linguistics,* Delta, NY, 7, 1966

15. Chomsky, N., *Syntactic Structures,* Mouton Press, The Hague, 1957

16. Postman and Weingartner, 65

17. Ibid., 102-103

18. Ibid., 103

19. Ibid., 103-104

Chapter Three
Learning to Write

Although the teacher's first concern is with the failure of young adults who enter graduate and post-graduate classes to use writing skills in a generative, communicational framework, this concern cannot be addressed in isolation. It implies some analysis of the kind of schooling they have received.

A persistent question intrudes. Why is it that infants find listening and speaking so easy to acquire, while reading and writing (writing more than reading) cause them so much grief, even when they start out on their quest of literacy at a young age, say four, well within the window of language opportunity claimed by nativists? Is one to assume that this native ability is for listening and speaking only (or at least primarily), and not for other manifestations of language?

In support of nativist arguments, it is fair to state that: (a) infants, even in non-conducive environments, do seem to pick up the basic elements of a language, provided they are exposed to it, (b) brain activity is remarkably energetic for the first few years of life, and (c) there is the phenomenon of quick acquisition of sign language in congenitally deaf infants, indicating that although the primary language organ is the ear, the eye can serve almost as well when it needs to do so. This is, of course, in children whose guardians have discovered early enough that they are deaf, and who make an effort to teach them. The problem with many disabled children is that guardians are not always aware of the disability until quite late.

Probably all the senses can be brought to serve the purpose of communication through language, if required. The sense of touch has enough powers of fine discrimination for blind learners to read through Braille. The senses of taste and smell play contributory roles, but in and of themselves are insufficiently discriminative for the subtle shades of language. This researcher is not aware of studies to determine if earlier or later exposure to Braille in a blind child makes any difference to the facility with which it is acquired, but if the nativist view is endorsed, early exposure should make it easier.

Normal children seem to be able to distinguish word boundaries in the continuous speech of adults, and to relate those sound groupings to meaning. In the phase of language acquisition that concerns Pakistanis, the transition to reading and writing involves a second transference and a second setting up of associations, this time of an entirely arbitrary sound-sense system (which have been associated with certain meanings) with a new set of entirely arbitrary symbols. When a child learns to write, a second complex process akin to but in many ways less natural than the first one, takes place.

Speech and conversation are 'situation' oriented,

that is, they derive much of their ongoing stimulus and support from the actual situation in which they occur. Confirmation and illustration of the spoken word is simultaneous, and in a continuous relationship with sensory reinforcement. The redundancies, repetitions and emphases of speech serve to clarify meaning, although the construction itself might be incomplete or faulty. And word selection in speech is usually within an often-used, ready-made speaking vocabulary. Speakers engaged in spontaneous conversation would probably not, or very rarely, use words like 'insofar' or 'nonetheless', even if they were learned persons.

English has developed quite a number (perhaps too many) punctuation marks, but writing really has very few props in the communicational complex. It has to carry the whole burden of meaning, clarification, communication, confirmation and illustration within itself. It is, perforce, more carefully constructed and complete than speaking. Since the writer has time to think, and does not have to make allowances for the immediate situation, he can choose his vocabulary more carefully. These factors make writing more difficult to decode than speaking. It tends to be 'non-situational'; the immediate confirmations of speaking are not available for the writer or his reader.

This is visible when people are forced into speaking situations that are really non-situational, news casting, for example, or public speaking. The ordinary props of conversation are no longer available. Most professional newscasters need the support of the 'non-situational' skills of reading and writing to bolster them as they go along. These used to come from notes lying in front of the newscaster, but are now supplied as a continuous frame of writing in front of the speaker, done to create the illusion that he is speaking, when, in fact, he is reading aloud. Likewise, orators and public speakers often need visual support from notes.

A child has already made one demanding intellectual effort to associate arbitrary sounds (there is nothing natural in any language about its selection of word-sounds for the things they represent) with meaning. Now he is asked to associate those sounds with arbitrary visual symbols. The *(object)-(sound)* relationship of a word has to be enlarged to include a new object, a complex set of arbitrary marks on a sheet of paper, so that it now becomes an *(object)-(sound)-(set of written symbols)* relationship. At some stage in the process, he has to transfer the object to the set of visual symbols with as little as possible of the intervening sound segment, especially if he is to become an efficient reader and writer.

Immature muscles are called upon to draw certain shapes. The process is not an exact or logical one. Writing in the phonetic alphabets, any of them, is a capricious business. English uses the Roman alphabet in a whimsical way. A child is supposed to understand (often by himself) that many of those shapes are merely suggestive of certain sounds, not fully and finally representative of them. The letter 'a', for example, does duty for nine or ten different straight vowel sounds and diphthongs in British English; if some American dialects are included there is yet another sound, a triphthong, while the Australians have a typical high nasalized and diphthongised version of some of these sounds. That makes twelve, thirteen or possibly more sounds for just one vowel, but when it is written it appears in only one form for all of them.

Learning to write in any *sound-symbol* system is difficult. English is especially difficult, but there are some perhaps even more so. For example, high level literacy in Chinese, where many ideas have to be interpreted individually in semantically rather than phonetically conceived graphemes, is said to require a lot of hard work, perhaps eighty years of it.

One part of the primary question as to why children who easily acquire oral skills often find it difficult to master writing skills is answered in the observations given above. Reading/writing involves a major second language effort while the child is still engaged in the perplexities of the first one. If one accepts the 'innate-ability' hypothesis, then a good bit of the native ability he possesses is already well extended in the recognition and interpretation of the sounds he hears around him, and it is strained yet more when he turns towards writing skills as well.

The problem is, if his exposure to written aspects of the language is deferred until he grows bigger, he will have lost a good bit of the brain's pristine energy, and the whole thing becomes more difficult. This is seen time and again in the failure, the high lapse rates or at best the marginal success, of many adult literacy programmes. It is a dilemma. Briefly stated, if the child is started off early he has a better chance of acquiring writing skills painlessly. However, if it is too soon, it might lead to a kind of linguistic 'overload' and prove to be self-defeating.

In general, regardless of the degree of truth in nativist arguments, they do not help the teacher very much in planning strategies for the teaching of writing.

If a mysterious inner power is at work in the brain of the infant, if he has some in-built Language Acquisition Device, one observes some apparent manifestations of its working with a sense of awe, one wonders at it, one might be able to talk and speculate about it, but there is not much one can do to tap its potential beyond exposing the child to written forms of the language, and hoping for the best.

Psychology

Implicit in this is the hurdle that psychology cannot be an exact science. At bottom it rests on two approaches; either the researcher 'looks into himself and assumes that his own internal processes are valid for other human beings, or he observes the external behaviour of people and infers internal processes from them. Either way, it is guesswork. He can never be sure. Looking into oneself is fraught with difficulties. It is arguable whether the brain can act on itself, and what a man's brain thinks it sees inside itself might be nothing more than what it wants to see. At the end of it, he can never really make a valid claim that what he thinks or feels is what other people think and feel also. Observing people might seem to be more tenable from a scientific point of view. However, a man may smile and smile and be a villain yet. Human beings are good at disguising their inner selves.

Behavioural psychologists tend to discount the nativist hypothesis. They point out that a lot of what goes on in the infant's early days fits well into their *stimulus-response-reinforcement* model of learning. Infants are encouraged in their efforts through immediate and joyous reinforcements from those around them, clapping, cries of appreciation, cuddling and kissing—an infant soon realises that it is doing something right. In Skinner's model of 'operant conditioning', undesired behaviour is ignored and steps in the direction of desired behaviour are reinforced through praise or reward (1).

The important points here are: (a) that learning is seen not as a finished product, but as a *process,* a movement through a series of connected stages towards a desired end. This movement can be random, as in 'trial-and-error' learning, which can waste a lot of time, or it can be guided and efficient, as in programmed learning. (b) that no punishment is given for undesired behaviour, and (c) that reinforcements are given immediately, as soon as each step in the process is accomplished successfully.

Deferring the reward might confuse the child, or make him think that something other than the desired end is important. Punishing a child for undesired behaviour might focus attention on *that* behaviour rather than on the desired one. It wastes time and vitiates the learning process. It is better to ignore it. A child will often do something he knows to be wrong in an effort to get attention. Attention is what he wants, whether it is of the loving kind or not. When he discovers that his wrong behaviour gets him nothing by way of attention or reward, it tends to wither away.

Two kinds of 'reinforcement' are identified. The first is a reward given as a smile, an embrace, or a sentence or two of praise (the more sincere the better). The second is the removal of an irksome burden, perhaps by letting the student go out of the classroom early. 'Punishment' is defined as *direct,* if a painful stimulus is added to the situation; and *indirect* if it is given as withholding a normally unpleasant expectation.

All 'reinforcement' or 'punishment' is not external. There are intrinsic patterns, as well, though behaviourists hesitate to assert anything about them because they are not visible or measurable. Individuals encourage themselves when they see themselves succeeding, as in suddenly understanding the point of a story, or in gaining an insight, or in learning the kind of muscular coordination needed for the performance of some desired activity. External reinforcement is unnecessary. They also punish themselves when they measure their own acquisitions or actions against those of their peers, or against inflexible criteria set out for them by parents or teachers. Some studies indicate that intrinsic rewards are more powerful than extrinsic ones. The self-motivated student is more effective than one who derives his effort from external stimuli (see M. Donaldson, *Children's Minds,* 1978, Fontana, and E.L. Deci, *Intrinsic Motivation,* 1975, Plenum Press, NY).

Whatever the truth of these recommendations (experimenters have been able to teach animals to do all sorts of things with these techniques), they have two advantages, (a) they deal with observable and measurable activities, and (b) they give the teacher something tangible to work with.

What concerns the teacher is that they are also far removed from the authoritarian model prevalent in Pakistan, where virtue is its own reward (good work is rarely praised) and error is immediately, sometimes gleefully, subjected to a series of harsh, 'corrective' measures.

Behavioural psychologists prefer to see the impressive language ability of the infant and young child less as the working of mysterious forces, and more as the result of massive positive reinforcement given at that stage. The average infant lives in a climate of encouragement. Every small achievement is greeted with loud and sustained expressions of approval. He learns in such a climate. Also, he wants to learn.

Two things happen as an infant grows older. By three or four, much of the early welcome is lost. Parents are exhausted and they might have other children to look after. The baby is no longer a cute little bundle of joy, but an active, fretful child, and its struggles to learn things no longer stimulate ecstatic approval in others. The natural climate of reinforcement previously enjoyed is progressively lost. Now there is censure and disapproval. This is always a trying stage in the development of a child. He becomes resentful and uncooperative, especially if he has to compete for attention with younger siblings who seem to get all the attention they want without effort.

The fall-out from this change can be debilitating from an educational point of view. Several reactions might result from it, but the dominant ones are (a) a withdrawal of effort and (b) dislike for the task in hand.

The second large event is the beginning of schooling. The child might have had a little exposure to written forms before he starts school, but the real beginnings of literacy are found here. Unfortunately, the beginnings of *il*literacy or *semi*-literacy are also found here. The difficulties of handwriting and spelling can be overwhelming. One talks about children: the fact is that many *adults* are unsure of their spelling. It may remain shaky even after years of effort, especially in an orthographic system as unphonetic and loosely defined as that of English.

These difficulties might impede any natural desire on the part of the child to communicate in writing. Traditional exercises at school substitute truly expressional assignments with the less demanding task of copying. The skills involved here are largely mechanical, and the evaluation of those skills tends to be in terms of the 'correct/incorrect' formulation discussed in the first chapter. This approach is popular because both the child and the teacher can work with tangibles, while the criteria for 'correct' forms are known and can be used without argument in the process of evaluation.

Yet language is basically an inventive, generative process, not a mechanical one. The skills of writing might be encouraged better if (a) the writing efforts of children were taken seriously, and (b) children were given a chance to find their own way from inside themselves in a series of growing, exploratory exercises rather than inflicting on them a series of copying exercises taken from sources outside themselves.

These skills would be reinforced by providing an environment of lavish praise, such as they enjoyed at home when they were learning to speak. Children would not only become better at writing, they would also *want* to write, and it is in that wanting that most of the battle is won. Motivation is fundamental to achievement and performance. The factors that encourage motivation are quick feedback, a feeling of success, an atmosphere of approval, and specific reinforcement. A motivated child will travel happily on a voyage of discovery through the seemingly endless complexities of spelling and syntax.

A new perspective on writing skills might emerge from such an approach. The author realises that this is somewhat Utopian (1). In the real world, one teacher dealing with fifty fractious children with short attention spans is more likely than not to resort to mechanical activities in which emphasis is given to correctness rather than communication, to forming letters correctly, and to copying. The end product of handwriting or sentence formation is put under the strictures of the 'correct/incorrect' neurosis. However, the expressional content of communication is not stimulated by forming written symbols correctly. A child might learn to form letters correctly, but this skill might not transfer itself to an ability to use the written medium for communication.

There are exceptions, of course, but the average school classroom in this country is not the best place for writing. Administrators and parents alike tend to demand that a teacher be able to maintain discipline. He becomes more like a policeman than an educator. Classrooms are expected to be sepulchres of silent learning. Students are not allowed to speak or question anything. From an administrative point of view, this is understandable, because one noisy class can disturb others in the immediate neighbourhood. Yet, desirable as this might be for other subjects, it tends to weaken the acquisition of language skills. A certain hubbub is part of the process. Continuous feedback is desirable, not only from the teacher but from the student's peers as well.

Writing is probably taught wrongly from the beginning. The activity is undertaken in isolation, with no appreciative audience to applaud the student as he masters each step in the complicated process. Feedback comes two or three days later on the finished product, from a grim-faced teacher who seizes upon things like spelling or handwriting to slash marks and castigate the student.

Later he will be asked to write about things like *A Trip To Murree* or *My Best Friend*. Ready-made essays on similar topics are found in grammar-composition books and commercial 'made-easies'. With a little intelligent manipulation they can be adapted to a variety of situations. Students find it more fruitful from an examination point of view to learn these essays by heart, than to use the language in a generative mode.

A few exceptional individuals will make the transference to communication. For most of the others the ordeal of writing is in reference to the 'reality' of the system, getting marks in tests. Short-cuts, rote-learning and ready-made applications are adopted. Most will remain at a quasi-mechanical level for several years, often well into adulthood. Sometimes all their lives, their responses will stay attuned to and inhibited by the 'correct/incorrect' fears inculcated in their educational psyche since their schooling days. Rare and cautious excursions might be made into expressional writing. Everything said here is exacerbated by an order of magnitude when it is the second rather than the first language. Generating language in English in writing is anathema for Pakistani students, no matter how ready they might be to use it in speech in whatever way they can.

Knowledge has a binary aspect, knowing *about* something and knowing *how to* do it. One is potential, and might never be manifested in the actual. The other is actual, and has little relationship with the potential. This is especially evident in language skills. One can know about something in an abstract way without being able to do it.

Conversely, one can know how to do something very well without knowing very much, or indeed anything, about it. This is precisely what a child of five or six does when he speaks. He assembles complex utterances, without knowing anything about nouns, verbs and adjectives. He is able to use grammatically subtle things like subjunctive and conditional forms, with no idea of what they are, moving from the concrete world around him into a world of hypothesis and supposition, an amazing feat performed with no theoretical knowledge whatsoever.

Observations like the foregoing have become truisms in linguistics, but educational planners are still found who insist on subjecting the child to academic knowledge about the language. This is the traditional way, supported by centuries of language teaching. It rests on the supposition that a practical skill will emerge from, and be improved by, academic insights. All evidence since the early part of the twentieth century indicates that this supposition is suspect, but it persists. During a language workshop held in Multan, one participant, a lady teacher in a local college spoke at considerable length with vehement finality on the need for strengthening the teaching of grammar at the college level to improve standards of English. She went away determined not to listen to any arguments against it. In the early nineteen eighties, this researcher was invited to give a talk on television. Before airing it, the Programme Producer excised those parts of the talk which questioned the role of traditional grammar. Later, when asked why he had done so, he said he was sure the author did not know what he was talking about

As mentioned in chapter one, abstract knowledge can inhibit performance by making the speaker, and even more than the speaker, the writer, self-conscious and anxious. It is precisely this that one should avoid. Teaching abstract knowledge might not just be useless, it might generate the very factors one wants to avoid: diffidence and evasiveness.

Teaching Writing

The teacher should be clear about his objectives in teaching writing. There is no question but that students should be able to write without worrying about the whys and wherefores. In all honesty, whether one ascribes to the cognitive school of thought or the behavioural, or a bit of both, no one really knows much about how the brain functions. This means that at this stage in human knowledge, it is foolhardy to make assertions about the brain, and even more so to base educational programmes committing students to this or that perception, on uncertain premises. The best on current offer is to provide an atmosphere of encouragement, and trust the inherent powers of the brain to make sense out of what it is trying to learn.

Writing should become something like speaking, a rapid, unselfconscious and confident transposition of ideation to language. More should go to the practice side of things, and less to the theoretical. There is a large element of habituation in the use of any language skill. The more the conscious process intrudes, the less likely will there be an easy, confident flow of language.

There is an autonomic 'repair' system in the use of each language skill. One hears it when a person says, '1 went there last Monday, I mean *Tuesday*,' (where he repairs 'fact' or 'data'), when he says, 'I ran over—ran *into*—Ahmed the other day' (where he repairs 'meaning') or when he says, 'If I had a million rupees I will, I mean 1 *would*, buy a big car' (where he repairs 'structure'). Other subtle repair jobs might also be undertaken, as when he has used an unnecessarily sharp or aggressive tone in a situation that does not warrant it. This indicates the presence of a self-watching system. The feedback is supplied from the self. In rapid speech a lot gets through because absolute precision is not vital to the needs of ordinary communication. Of course, where it is vital, as in a lawyer arguing a case, the self-monitor would be careful. But most of the time it is unobtrusively vigilant, without being dictatorial.

It tends to be sharply and obtrusively vigilant in writing, which is a permanent and irrefutable record of one's linguistic misdeeds and ideational poverty. It can so stultify the process that hardly any writing is ventured at all. A self-monitoring mechanism develops naturally for all the skills, and is an essential component in language acquisition. However, it seems to develop into something overwhelming for the writing skill.

To apportion blame, one has to look away from 'nature' towards 'nurture'. Whatever the innate ability of human beings to listen and speak (and perhaps read and write as well), writing rests heavily on 'nurture'. The finger of blame points at the attitudes and approaches of traditional teachers, who are entrenched and confident in those attitudes and approaches in the first instance, and to a society at large whose own expectations are conditioned by the same attitudes and approaches, in the second.

A baby struggling to form words with immature speech

muscles is rarely subjected to criticism for mistakes he might make. However, absolute precision is demanded in writing right from the beginning, and the motivational framework of this demand is punitive, setting up all sorts of fears and anxieties, which the individual carries over into adult life.

Generally, the teaching effort should be to motivate students towards individual expression and personal responsibility. It should also be extremely tolerant towards failure or slow production.

This is what Holdaway says:

> 'If there is anything we have a responsibility towards as adults and academics, it is the complex fabric of intellect and emotion which characterises human learning, human endeavour and human beingness. It is easy to sit in smug intellectual superiority from which we have taken a wealth of hidden satisfaction, and damn those who cannot learn without emotional support. In so doing we are, in the face of our own experience of success and pleasure, denying the deeply affective nature of learning. There is no such thing as human insight without human emotion.'(3)

The implications of the tension line should be understood, as it affects the learner. Unless one can allow him a meaningful context of expression, one should not do anything with him at all. It is the classic case of the caring, pro-active, conscientious 'good' teacher becoming the 'bad' teacher by fussing and fretting around the student too much. In the observation of learning and performing a skill, one discovers, first, that one knows very little about how it comes about, and second, that different people have different strategies. Typical cognitive or mechanistic theories fall short in their descriptions. There are many uncharted roads to Xanadu; and there are also some promising pathways that never quite get there. The learner might take knowledge from one skill and apply it to another. The teacher does not know from which source the learner's successful strategies might spring. There is some sense in integrating the skills of language, but this should not be in a strictly guided teaching format. The teacher's main challenge in writing is to awaken the student's communicational mode (which he already has in speaking) in writing. Success, it seems, is more strongly defined when it emerges from the student's own strivings. It has little to do with this or that teaching method.

Developmental patterns are time-and-place constrained. It is self-defeating to expect a certain level of performance associated with a more advanced stage of the process, at a less advanced stage. Parents and teachers who proudly display 'prodigies', little mites who can lisp a few poems, or play the piano, or write their own names correctly while their 'less-talented' peers tumble around breaking things, might be harming them. One says 'might', because one does not really know. The adulation a child receives for unexpectedly advanced performance may reinforce the achievement; conversely, it may help to freeze it at the wrong place in the sequence of maturation, or at the wrong moment in time, or to generate an unreal frame of expectation. It is better if a child can work from things he feels to be his strengths towards things he is less certain about.

Some room should be given to the child to work out his own strategies. This entails a teaching mode that does not teach in the formal sense, or that teaches in that sense as little as possible. TTT (teacher talking time) should be within a five to fifteen per cent band of the total time available for a writing class. This will be taken up later in the section of this study on practical classroom techniques. It should be remembered that most of the discussion in this chapter is in reference to young children, but only because what happens to them may be relevant to what they can or cannot do later as young adults.

The teacher's warmly confident assistance in addressing some of these hurdles is crucial. As far as possible it should be assistance, not correction. In other words the student should be encouraged to find solutions for his own problems. His struggles and failures should not provide the teacher with an occasion for generating tension and fear for the student in being exposed to ridicule or censure in front of everyone.

With regard to the receptive, parallel skill of reading, one commentator has the following to say:

> '...At first the child is producing a message from his oral language experience and a context of past associations. He verifies it as probable or improbable in terms of these past experiences and changes the response if the check produces uncertainty....At some time during the first year at school visual perception

begins to provide some cues but for a long period these are piecemeal, unreliable and unstable. This is largely because the child must learn where and how to attend to print. Slowly the first sources of cues from experience and from spoken language are supplemented by learning along new dimensions, such as letter knowledge, word knowledge, letter-sound associations and pronounceable clusters of letters. As differences within each of these dimensions gradually become differentiated the chances of detection and correction of error are increased...' (4)

The impression given by the foregoing is of a rising pattern of discrimination and approximation *within* the student, drawn initially in comparison with knowledge he already has, and moving gradually away into new fields. The point to be stressed here is that this is something inside him. Although the source for the receptive skills, both of them, is external (except when the subject communes with himself, the source for listening is someone else speaking, and in reading it is someone else who has written something down), the skill itself is internal. He experiments, recreates, rejects, accepts and validates his own acquisitions and judgements from resources inside himself. This seems to be the natural way, the way the brain is equipped to function in its quest for understanding and knowledge.

What seems true for the receptive skills is even more strongly registered with the productive skills. The natural source is internal rather than external.

It is less natural when his attention is forced in the direction of quantities to be learnt within arbitrary time-frames imposed from the outside. Perhaps a good way of teaching writing is to give the student a pencil, and ask him to doodle and scribble in whatever fashion he wants, until he is ready to take off, and then to let him go in whatever direction he wishes, applauding him when he seems to be getting things together, and ignoring his mistakes.

The theory is good, but in fact a lot of motivation is supplied by external sources. There are very few 'self-starters' in this business. Most students expect guidance and reinforcement, and this expectation is stronger in second language learning. A teacher who assigns his students a writing task without telling them what to write about, will probably get very little in return.

If it is decreed by an arbitrary syllabus that the student, *shall* learn fifty simple past and simple present tense expressions during the first term, and that he will get good marks if he can demonstrate his familiarity with them and that those marks are what he will be evaluated by, then he will probably learn those fifty expressions. If he knows that his parents will be pleased if he gets good marks, a framework of external and not always relevant compulsions will be grafted on to the natural learning process. It might distort it.

He can certainly learn what his teachers tell him to learn, especially if he understands that it is important to his teachers or parents that he does so. He can get good marks. But will what he learns be transferred to an ability to use the language spontaneously and creatively? The mass of evidence lying in front of teachers in Pakistan, suggests that the transference is too often incomplete, and nearly always inadequate.

Left to himself in good measure, if not entirely, he would probably learn to use visual forms of the language more efficiently, and in a more truly communicational mode, by unconsciously employing the internal categories just mentioned. The teacher might meddle to weaken and confuse those categories, not strengthen them.

Some extreme positions should be noted. Some decades ago there was a ten year experiment in total student-centrism in the Sri Aurobindo Asharam in India. No syllabus was prescribed and no regular class held, leaving students to decide what, how and when they would study. However, at the end of this experiment it was recommended that syllabuses, regular classes and tests be reintroduced as they helped to circumscribe areas of learning, set up patterns of habituation and provide reasonably clear goals.

Experiments of this nature represent a kind of unguided 'process' approach. That they reverted to formalistic norms is interesting. The reasons for the reversion probably emerge from social rather than educational imperatives. How is a prospective employer to judge that a student knows his subject if there is no goal-oriented planning, no curricular organisation and no evaluative certification? Too much is left to the whims and subjective judgement of teachers. The pressures of the job market demand an organised, verifiable, reliable answer to the questions raised here.

The other extreme of the 'process' approach is the strictly defined, guided and straight-jacketed input of programmed learning. The skill acquiring process is analysed carefully. Every step is precisely metered towards a certain objective within a ladder of objectives. These objectives are stated in behavioural, visible, testable terms, so that both student and teacher can see clearly if the objective has, or has not, been achieved.

The thing is controlled at all points, but then the student is left to his own devices. Carefully formatted study material is supplied to him in incremental stages, until he reaches the overall goal defined for the material. It is formulated in such a way that he will be more likely to succeed than to fail at each step, and his success is rewarded by confirming it, by giving the answer immediately, or by delaying it slightly, perhaps by putting it at the end or upside down at the bottom of the page or even by hiding it until the next frame emerges, thus motivating him to move forward. The hope of this approach is that the brain will systematically collect all those successful little steps and fuse them into an understanding of the whole thing.

In practice it was found that while these techniques proved effective for training animals in the performance of simple physical tasks, human subjects tended to get bored by a series of automatically 'right' answers, and to then do the whole thing rather superficially. Also, the gains tended to be short lived, a case of 'easy-come-easy-go.' Delaying the reinforcement helped in fixing the item in the brain. However, delaying the reinforcement could also lead to fixing the item at the wrong place in the sequence.

Programmed learning is now less popular than it was in the sixties and seventies. There was a spate of programmes for all sorts of things, including writing.

Most computer courses are programmed. Somehow, the concept never quite fulfilled its promise as anticipated.

One reason might be the *gestalt* proclivity of the brain to move from wholes to parts rather than the other way around. This was established by the Gestalt-psychologists in the nineteen twenties and thirties through extensive experimentation, and nothing much has happened since then to question the validity of their findings. Basically, people perceive form before they perceive detail. Also, they try to 'close' or complete perceptions when they are incomplete. This is the important psychological basis of 'cloze' type exercises and tests. Human beings look for complements because the mind needs patterns and closures to arrange things into meaningful wholes.

Another reason is that natural learning is rarely *linear* in the way described in simple programmed instruction. Proponents of this practical model of learning became aware of it and offered different kinds of programmes. *Branching* programmes were introduced which enabled people to ignore items they did not need to learn, or to get additional information in difficult areas. *Adjunct* programmes assumed a level of knowledge in advance and attempted to build onward from there. The idea of *mathetics,* or non-linear or reverse movement, was also entertained. The brain jumps around from one thing to another, looking for areas to which it can relate in terms of what it already knows, so that what it is trying to comprehend begins to make sense. It might start its learning somewhere in the middle, rather than in the beginning. It might want to move both forwards and backwards, separately or simultaneously. It might pick out recognisable points which provide learning anchors all over the place, and then try to fill in missing areas later. It might even go backwards from the end to the beginning. Human beings have restless, grasshopper brains that work best when they are free to work as nature intended them to work, and that baulk when they are artificially canalised.

A third reason for the indifferent success of this model could be that the whole thing tends to be externally, rather than internally, oriented. Yet another reason is the insistence on treating a language as a subject like other subjects. Visible here is a rejection, or at best, a guarded acceptance, of the cognitive assumption that there is a Language Acquisition Device, a specific learning faculty or facility for language, as separate from a general learning ability. One recalls the old debate as to whether there is a diffused G-factor or general intelligence available in the brain for learning all things, or specialised abilities and faculties for learning specific things.

The Brain

Behaviourists tend to be timid about asserting or denying anything to do with the internal working of the brain because it cannot be seen or measured except in superficial ways. Recent hopes that Magnetic Resonance Imaging or Positron Emission Tomography would reveal this inner working have remained largely unrealized, though some progress has been made. The brain uses about the same energy as a twenty-watt bulb when it is working, but apparently it does not heave or writhe or pump blood or get detectably hot or move around at all. Nor does it set up an electric firework display. Tests of its assumed electrical activity are inconclusive. The mechanistic picture of the brain is of an electrically energised, computer-like switchboard of immense complexity. But this electrical energy might be a manifestation of its working, not a cause of it. One can sometimes see the end product of the brain's working; but until observational techniques improve, one has to remain unsure about how it goes about doing what it does.

It does not have one way, but a multiplicity of ways. Separate parts control separate functions, but there is also a marked degree of interchangeability and plurality in its make-up. It talks to itself and about itself, and confirms new items in the light of what it has already stored. It tests, accepts or rejects things against a self-established frame of criteria in a continuous flurry of activity.

It is an awe-inspiring organ. However, say the behaviourists, it is certainly a physical organ and should, therefore, be subject to the physical laws of nature. Mysterious inner faculties, they say, cannot be assumed until they are confirmed.

In the non-mentalist view of things, language is not given any special status. An hour or so is allocated out of the daily time-table for the 'subject' called English. Nevertheless, that a language is not a subject like, say, Physics, should be clear on reflection. It is too much a part of the very web and woof of a person to be treated separately. It is not itself a subject, it is the tool whereby the individual attempts to understand other subjects and the world around him. While some of the empiricism of Physics might seep into his attitudinal modalities to make him a little less irrational than he is, it does not become tightly fused to, or the very basis of, his thinking and feeling in the way a language does. A language is not a given corpus of so much knowledge stored somewhere in the brain. It is a growing, generative capability; it is the very foundation of thought and knowledge.

There is a dilemma for the teacher. The cognitive arguments raise an intuitively confirmatory response, especially with regard to language, but they do little to suggest workable and defensible patterns of teaching and learning. However, the patterns suggested by the behaviourists, which seem to be more productive in that they are definable and defensible, often fall short of what the teacher might want, especially in writing. And in most teaching activities, little time is given to the understanding of the emotional substratum of learning.

The foregoing arguments indicate the need to recognise that emotional, cognitive and behavioural elements, all go into the making of the learning complex. A sensitive teacher might be able to help with emotional factors. Cognitive factors do not lend themselves to empirical validation, but something in the learning cycle should be left for these factors—since so little is known about their working, it is probably better not to try and guide or canalise them too much. With regard to behavioural elements, the teacher can do quite a lot, but he has to be careful not to overlook the other factors. Most language courses tend to become primarily mechanistic in overall conceptualisation, administration and evaluation.

According to Holdaway:

> 'The rhythm of challenge, effort, and reward is so fundamental to learning—indeed, to every few seconds of human endeavour—that

to overlook it is to invite failure. Sadly, when we are concerned with literacy learning, we are frontally concerned with failure, ineptitude, defeat, inferiority, despair, and the terrifying injustice of finding yourself left behind. As teachers or academics most of us don't recognise this because we were the ones who weren't. Our competence rests on our ability to be sufficiently on top of the ball game to have gained pleasure from every stroke. Learning is always a question of emotional rewards, of awareness of success, of progressively achieving cognitively ratifiable advances.'(5)

Summary

From the sum of arguments in this and the previous chapter, a system in which the student's internal mechanism is permitted to function, which is 'age-appropriate' rather than obsessed with performance, which makes allowances for individual variation, which is 'skill and tool' oriented rather than end-product oriented, and which is not distorted by the tension pall of examinations and the whole unhappy social complex of 'correct/incorrect' or 'pass/fail' neuroses, is probably the best for creating a climate of real skill acquisition at school. This is especially desirable for the productive skills.

The exceptional student will vault these impediments and get to where he wants to go, but it is unfair to strew the path with impediments, even for such as him. In any case, he is a rarity. The teacher's concern is with the average student who should be liberated from the fear of ridicule-inducing failure, or he will never flourish. It might be difficult to adjust to such an attitudinal change. There is a tendency to use fear as a bludgeon to force conformity in this society. Schools that 'go-easy' on the student, that actually try and make it a place of pleasure and reward for him, are frowned upon by parents and authorities alike. Even so, grudging adjustments have taken place elsewhere in the world. It should not be impossible to make a few here as well. This researcher is not aware of the existence of schools which operate on these norms in Pakistan. Expensive private schools are as inextricably linked to the marks-and-result compulsions as the much cheaper public ones. What they send to higher classes is a student, very often with extremely high marks, who has no confidence in his ability to write, who is panic-stricken if asked to suggest ideas about mundane topics, and whose internalised skill structure with regard to the flexible, creative use of language is still unformed.

Chapter 3 End Notes

1. Skinner, B., "A Functional Analysis of Verbal Behaviour" (1957), in *The Psychology of Language, Thought and Instruction,* ed., De Cecco, Holt, Rinehart and Winston, London, 1970, 318-325

2. See Donaldson, M., *Children's Minds,* Fontana, 1978, and Deci, E., *Instrinsic Motivation,* Plenum Press, NY, 1975

3. Holdaway, D., *The Foundations of Literacy,* Ashton Scholastics, Sidney, Auckland, NY, Toronto, London, 1979, 98

4. Clay, M., *Reading, the Patterning of Complex Behaviour,* Heinemann Educational Books, Auckland, 1972, 161-162

5. Holdaway, 97

Chapter Four
Some Aspects of Pakistani English

Pakistan has evolved its own dialects of English. They are insular in that they are not readily amenable to remediation, at least this author has not found them to be so. By a 'dialect' he means a fairly complete system with enough by way of internal resources to act as a viable tool of communication, yet which is sufficiently different from related systems to warrant recognition in its own right. In the case of English, there is a world-wide collection of ideolects and dialects. The term is sometimes used interchangeably with 'accent', which relates primarily to sound systems. However, the connotation adopted here is broader,

No dialect is better or worse than any other. There is no such thing as one correct dialect of English and several incorrect ones. However, it is also possible for one or some dialects to wander so far from other dialects with worldwide recognition, such as British or American ones, that it becomes difficult to add them to the general family tree. Problems exist even for the two main sets of dialects:

> The complexities of the English language are such that even native speakers cannot always communicate effectively, as almost every Briton learns on his first day in America. Indeed, Robert Birchfield, editor of the Oxford English Dictionary, created a stir in linguistic circles on both sides of the Atlantic when he announced his belief that American English and English English are drifting apart so remorselessly that one day the two nations may not be able to understand each other at all...(1)

Linguistic studies have helped to broaden attitudes with regard to language. Elitist views are no longer tenable, though they are surprising tenacious in Pakistan. This is one of the many contradictory pressures that students encounter. The English they learn is not British English, yet their output continues to be judged by British English. Old colonial Received Pronunciation is nowadays hardly heard anywhere, even in its country of origin, yet it continues to beleaguer spoken dialects of English in countries such as Pakistan. It still hovers in the background of a society where what passes for written English is now far removed indeed from those British models. This did not seem to matter some years ago when Pakistanis were content to go galloping along in their markedly deviant dialects of English, and little was done to discourage them. This was the patriotically assertive 'English-is-not-our-language-and-we-shall-mess-around-with-it-as-much-as-we-want' phase in the shifting fortunes of this language over the last six decades in this country, which has witnessed several changes of government, each determined to undo the policies of the previous one. Educational institutions have been privatised or nationalised, centralised or decentralised, 'Urduised' or 'Englishised' according to the political whim of the moment-- no policy has really had a chance to take root. More recently, however, people have become aware of its growing importance, and have begun to regret its gradual loss in educational circles. Now English is required for all sorts of things within the country and abroad. Striving to maintain international standards can be supported by good arguments, many of which relate to globalization.

Over the last fifty years or so, American English has pretty much succeeded in pushing British English out of the top slot. Insisting on the South East dialect of Britain as the 'standard' of English is now rather silly, since American forms are invading British ones in some areas of usage and spelling. The process is hastened by the ubiquitous computer and its dominantly 'American' vision, so that more and more pieces written in English now appear with American spelling or idiom. This does not matter to the average third-world student.

Pakistani English

A glance at the linguistic map of Pakistan reveals that about seventy languages are spoken in the country. Some, such as Urdu and to a lesser degree English, are spread across most parts of the country, others, such as Punjabi, Sindhi, Pushto and Balochi are confined to large tracts of land and are spoken in significant numbers, while many are confined to small areas and are spoken by a few people in relatively remote parts of the country. English is never included among Pakistani languages, yet it is one of the most important languages in the country. It is found everywhere. If someone sets up a small business he will quite unconsciously give it an English name. If he paints a board for his shop he will automatically do it in English. His accounting will be done in English and he will not think it strange that the numbers he uses are always the English ones, not the Urdu ones. All banking, invoicing and ordering will be done in English. Most of his records will be kept in English. At the same time he might never need to speak the language. Of course there are exceptions, but this indicates how deeply and widely this language has permeated the day-to-day writing transactions of this society. It is time to include English among Pakistani languages, but with the caveat that this is Pakistani English and not American or British English. The original model of the language was British English, especially the dialect spoken and written by the ruling elite of Britain. No other model was in a position to offer serious competition at the time. However, regardless of models and the efforts of British rulers, Pakistani English has gone its own way. This is what the earliest writer in this field, Dr Tariq Rahman, has to say about it:

' ...before 1984 the term PE (Pakistani English) was almost unknown and the assumption in English speaking circles was that educated Pakistanis use BSE (British Standard English). All deviations from it were considered mistakes and once people were made aware that a feature of their writing was Pakistani, they tried to avoid it altogether. In 1984 college and university lecturers began to be trained in teaching English as an international language in Islamabad every year. Now there is some awareness that there are non-native varieties of English, though in private conversation people still manifest prejudice against PE and consider it only incorrect English...' (2)

There is some reluctance among teachers and administrators to recognize these developments. However, at some stage they will have to be faced. There is a well established and stubborn entity called Pakistani English (or Pinglish as some people call it, usually with a self-deprecatory grin). It refuses to go away. Do we accept it, teach it and, above all, *assess* our students according to it, or do we continue to strain after the mirage of British English? If we accept it, a lot of descriptive and pedagogical work will have to be done. Dictionaries will have to be written, syllabuses will have to be revised, study material will have to be developed and teachers will have to be retrained. At the end of it students and parents might resent the fact that 'substandard' English was being taught at educational institutions. The matter is still uncertain.

Second Language Interference on Itself through the First language

Everybody knows about first language interference on the second language. However, the second language also penetrates the first language in a distorted way and then impinges on itself. In seeping through Urdu or other Pakistani languages, English emerges from the other end in a new form. Uncountable numbers of English expressions have slipped into Pakistani Urdu (Indian Urdu might not be equally affected) and have Anglicised the parallel Urdu expressions to some extent. In the process they have also been Urduised to a visible extent. English terms are used in abundance in modern Pakistani Urdu; a few people insist on pronouncing them in an 'English' way, even when they are speaking Urdu, e.g. 'BALcony' instead of 'balCONY'. Such people are oddities. Most people use them in an 'Urdu' way, and might not be aware that they are of English origin, just as they would probably not be aware of the origin of the numerous Arabic and Persian words they use, or the Portuguese origin of words like 'peepa' (cannister), 'saabon' (soap) or 'chhaapna' (to print). When local speakers use English words in their Urdu communication, as all of them do, the dominant perception remains Urdu-like rather than English-like. When they use English, as many of them need to do, they continue with the Urdu way of things. In Anglicising Urdu, English has succeeded in Urduising itself. The villain of the piece is transliteration, which is done blindly in administrative and commercial circles all over the country. English is spoken in an Urdu way because English words are seen and pronounced in an Urdu way when they are written in the Urdu script. Speaking difficulties certainly exist, but it is really writing that affects the process.

This has been going on for well over a century. Even when the British were here, the English used by locals had its own flavour. The author sees no way of reversing or changing something so deeply entrenched. Local dialects of English began to form right from the beginning of the British period in this part of the subcontinent--about a century and a half ago. Whatever we do for the language today will have to take some of these observations into account (3).

English is no longer the prestige language of Pakistan. It has become the primary source of development, commerce, internationalism, procedure and information. However, the views of those who see it as an undesirable relic of colonialism should not be ignored. There is an undercurrent of resentment against the language, especially among those who have not had the advantage of good schooling and exposure. It is an urban phenomenon that has left the vast rural population relatively untouched. This, too, is blatantly discriminatory and needs to be addressed properly. Briefly, if English is good for one Pakistani, it should be equally good for all Pakistanis. The answer to 'what kind of English' will have to wait. The country is not psychologically ready for Pakistani English. At the same time it is not good at International Standard English (some people argue hotly that no such thing exists).

What this nation probably needs is some kind of bi-dialectism, the ability to function in different modes of English as the situation demands. This would entail being able to use the Pakistani English set of dialects within Pakistan, and the International Standard English set of dialects, British or American, elsewhere. This is a big order.

1. Bryson, B., Ibid. 2

2. Rahman, T., *Pakistani English,*
    Vanguard, Islamabad, 1990, 1-2

3. Morphological and syntactic deviations abound
    in Pakistani English. Many examples are given
    by Baumgardner (1987: 241-252), others by
    Rahman for different dialects of Pakistan English
    (1990: 42-61). Some are also noted in modules
    developed for the distance teaching programme of
    the Allama Iqbal Open University between 1979
    and 1981 by this author (*Postgraduate Diploma
    Course in English Language Teaching,* Course No
    515, Units One, Two, Nine and Ten, AIOU) and
    yet others will be found in *Remaking English in
    Pakistan* (2004, NUML, Islamabad), also by this
    author. A great deal more needs to be done

Chapter Five
The Tools of Writing

Primary Difficulties

Whatever should or should not have happened at school, the university teacher has to make do with the following countdown of skills in English among the majority of his students: (i) *listening skills,* fairly well developed, provided a limited vocabulary is used; (ii) *reading skills,* fairly well developed; (iii) *speaking skills,* adequate for ordinary communication, though heavily Pakistanised in stress, intonation, rhythm and sound production, usually within the range described as the *mesolect* by Rahman; (iv) *writing skills,* consistently poor—all kinds of error are encountered, but the most common are seen in articles, tenses, number, agreement, word order, question formation, conditionals, spelling, punctuation, genitives and vocabulary.

Some examples taken from student assignments are given below:

1. '( )Brain is () physical organ, whereas () mind is () totality of brain( )s functioning...' (articles missing: possessive of brain shown without an apostrophe).

2. 'Lady Macbeth *driving his* husband to *commit* () *murder* of ( ) *king...*' (incomplete continuous aspect, the simple present would have been better; 'his' husband and 'her' wife are seen frequently and are a take-off from the Urdu way of marking the gender of the thing possessed in the possessive pronoun, rather than that of the possessor; also, 'murder the king' would have been better—the complexities introduced here are unnecessary. As an extension of this trend, most students feel they must say 'the English language' or 'the Urdu language' [often without the determiner], instead of just 'English' or 'Urdu'. Likewise, one comes across many instances of anxious detailing, such as 'He (Chaucer) talks about him (the Squire)...').

3. 'He made himself pregnant with ideas' (this sort of thing happens when students strain for effect. The idea is to bludgeon the examiner into doling out marks by using what students call 'bombastic' words).

4. 'Chaucer *used* his keen observational powers and *draws* a telling portrait of a knight, who *represented* the dying chivalric age...' (we see a double tense change in a single statement. This is, of course, possible, but it makes for confusing reading).

5. 'He asked him why *should he go* when there was so much danger...' (When asked, most students know the rule for the formation of questions in direct or indirect speech, but knowing the rule does not seem to help)

6. 'Chaucer does not offer harsh criticism, but *give* us good-humourly pen-sketches of various characters...'(mixing the negative and affirmative with the same subject leads to anomalies in verb agreement like this one; 'good-humourly' is an unknown adverb used as an adjective here. Unfortunately, though the suffix 'ly' is a common marker of the adverb, English also has adjectives like 'bodily', 'ugly' and 'lovely' to further confuse foreign learners).

7. 'If he *would* study hard, he *would have been* a good student. (This construction was produced because, unfortunately, too much crowding of instruction was undertaken by the author. The conditionals of English are not structured in the same way as those of Urdu. Trying to condense too much into one session can be counterproductive. Since skill acquisition is a matter of habit formation, adequate time is needed for assimilation).

8. (New sentence) '...he writes in *a* Middle English Tongue but this is not Difficult to understand in the *modren* (common Pakistani spelling) Times once we *understand* it and is known as ( ) Father of English poetry...(only about a fifth of the original rambling, spasmodic statement has been

shown here; Urdu does not use capital letters or punctuation marks, apart from a dash and an occasional question mark, nor is its paragraph conceived or structured in the same way as the English one; odd omissions or insertions of capital letters [though why capitals should be used at all is difficult to explain, except through some process of hypercorrection] and wayward punctuation can occur when Urdu is taken as the source model).

9. He asked; '*Why you waste* time learning Mongolian? You *should better* spend your time learning useful world language *like* English or French...' (questions are formed differently in Pakistani English; at least two deviations are seen in the second statement— 'you should better' is a common Pakistani blend of 'you had better' and 'should,' while 'useful world language' would need the indefinite article, which is missing here. The author would prefer 'such as' to 'like' in this example. 'Like' is more appropriate when a comparison is taking place, and 'such as' is better when introducing examples. However, one can quibble too much. Young Pakistanis have started to sprinkle 'like' all over the place—'He is, *like,* my friend, but only when I am, *like*, helping with his homework...' This a new kind of filler, used in place of the 'ers' and 'umps' of the older generation.

Attitudes

The primary effort should be to get students out of the

Urdu mould, though not entirely (they are already literate in one language). And the primary tools for improving writing must be placed squarely in the affective domain. The researcher has noticed that simply telling students seems to help in a small way. Many of them are anxious to improve their English, but are not aware that most of the trouble has been caused by Urdu. A firm stand that all thinking and writing should henceforth be in English, might cause some difficulty and resentment in the beginning. However, if the teacher continues to insist that flexible expression in English is one of the requirements of evaluation, and if he refuses to accept sloppy expression or phrases learnt by heart from other sources, a strong upward suction can be generated. This is best when it is accompanied by showing them how the Urdu language does things and how different this can be from the English language's way of doing the same things, without, of course, suggesting that either is superior to the other.

Senior students are not usually satisfied with blind instruction, and look for reasons as well. However, too much Urdu is not desirable. As a medium of explanation, it should not be used at all. As a framework of comparison, it should be used minimally and very carefully. One will occasionally come across a student who thinks his construction is the correct one, and will cite an Urdu example in support of his contention. Patience has to be shown when this happens. At one seminar, a Pakistani teacher of English claimed that the RP accent of a good British speaker on the dais was 'Cockney,' when in fact it wasn't. People tend to take themselves as touchstones of rightness in assessing things, especially with regard to language. Likewise, an Anglo-Pakistani, speaking very fluently but in what used to be called the 'chi-chi' accent some years ago, an accent characterised by a certain lilt, tight vowels, diminished diphthongs and some retroflex consonants, was heard asserting that English people no longer knew how to speak English.

The teacher comes up against entrenched language patterns supported by the structural formation of the source language. In attitudes he might encounter disbelief, nationalistic resentment, or simply student pragmatism. It requires a high degree of commitment on his part to deal with all this, specifically and generally. It is especially difficult to deal with it under the shadow of approaching examinations when getting good marks assumes priority over all else, no matter how idealistic the teacher or student might otherwise be.

Writing

Without a doubt, many of the basics of writing are ignored or taught badly in most schools in the country. There is probably no escape from a 'back to basics' approach, even at the highest level. For two reasons the approach would certainly need to be more sophisticated, one because a lot of what is done will be covertly corrective in nature, rather than overtly formative, adding another dimension to the task; and two because at this level the subjects are adults with well-formed minds of their own. Changing habits is always more difficult than forming them.

Although the difficulties mentioned in the first part of this chapter are grammatical in nature, it is felt that merely returning to a recital of rules will not do much for the student. It might be possible to by-pass these problems by keeping the focus away from them.

Writing offers an especially powerful medium of expression because of its comparative permanence, its measured feed-back and its opportunities for deliberation, selection and correction. Clearly, motivational factors in the affective domain must receive primacy in remediation. Some of these factors will be discussed in chapter five.

The trend of argument so far has been to remove as many of the tensions associated with writing as possible. For adults, as for children, writing provides a medium of self-expression that transcends the volatility and evanescence of speech. If the adult can overcome the psychological hurdles produced by years of schooling he may find in writing the essence of a lot of self understanding.

The desire for self-expression is strong. People want to explore the self and say something with a degree of permanence beyond that of speaking, which contains some meaning for themselves and perhaps for others as well. It is better if the criteria as to what is writable come from within. However, adult students joining a writing course or endeavouring to improve their writing ability between full time courses in literature or other advanced subjects will look to their teachers for guidance, at least in the beginning. With small children it is possible, even desirable, to give them pencil and paper and ask them to get on with whatever they want to do, scrawl, draw pictures, make line patterns all over the sheet, or try forming a few words or write stories that appeal to them, all in an atmosphere of approval and encouragement. With adults a greater degree of guidance is indicated, though the pedagogical elements will remain essentially the same.

Whether productive or receptive, language is an effort to organise personal meaning. This may be in emotions, physical sensations, ideas, images, rhythms or sounds, and non-verbal factors can greatly enrich the process. Who has not experienced the emotional let-down which comes from reading simplified or modernised texts of their favourite authors? For the productive skills of speaking and writing, the stronger the semantic impetus, the more focused and forceful is the expression likely to be.

Some categories can be suggested for the purposes and functions of language. Communication is only one aspect of it, and there are expressive functions of language which might have little to do with communication between persons. For example, a person might wait until he is alone to express his real emotions. People often indulge in personal and private discourse, or they might take pleasure in the non-representative aspects of a poem beyond what it seems to be trying to say, just as it is possible to derive pleasure and something close to 'meaning' from a piece of instrumental music accompanied by no words, whatsoever. Music and singing are forms of communication with very little or no representational element—the semantic content of most songs is trivial and secondary to the sound effects of words. They might, in fact, project no meaning at all in a formal sense.

Even between people, what is called phatic communion has little reference to meaning as such. When one person greets another with statements of the obvious about the weather, it has nothing to do with useful information about the weather, but everything to do with a willingness to acknowledge and befriend the other person. If one takes the modern facility of chat-mail for the last, writing can perform similar functions, though in a more delayed manner

The Purposes of Writing

Language and writing might be conceived somewhat differently by children and adults. The general functions of language relate to public communication, private expression, private thought and language satisfaction, by which is meant the pleasure, both public and private, which is derived from the language itself. According to Britton, speech functions in primary school children centre on the self and have a strong expressional content, so that:

> ...the earliest forms of written speech are likely
> for every reason to be expressive.(l)

This echoes a well-known position that the earliest form of adult writing was probably 'poetic' rather than 'prosaic', an assumption that may or may not be true. Underlying it is the belief that early people were primitive, and that 'primitive' equates with 'childish', an inference that has little support from what fragments of knowledge have come down from pre-history about such people.

Mundane imperatives to keep records and maintain accounts probably spurred the development of 'objective' writing in many early cultures. However, the assumption might contain a grain or two of truth—underdeveloped societies even today tend to be more 'poetic' than developed ones. The poet is still honoured much more than record keepers or objective scholars in such societies.

Children are natural poets. The transition to objective writing is slow, and not always successful.

According to Halliday,

> Language is 'defined' for the child by its uses; it is something that serves this set of needs... For the child, all language is doing something: in other words, it has meaning. It has meaning in a very broad sense, including here a range of functions which the adult does not normally think of as meaningful...it is precisely in relation to the child's conception of language that it is most vital for us to redefine our notion of meaning; not restricting it to the narrow limits of representational meaning (that is, content) but including within it all the functions that language has as a purposive...

In Halliday's view, the definition of meaning should be widened beyond representation and communication to include the fulfillment of functions. The relevance of this observation is not confined to oral language at school. It is true of a lot of writing in the adult world. Advertising rests heavily on the first three categories, and has little to do with representation; signs and notices have a basically regulative function, while manuals and books of instruction cater to the heuristic function.

(Note: It is not clear to the researcher if prevarication and the deliberate use of language to mystify listeners or readers and obscure meaning, fit into any of Halliday's categories. Some sort of indirect regulatory function is implied, using language to prevent unwanted actions or reactions, or to escape a difficult situation, or to create a linguistic smoke screen. Children learn quite early that *suppressio verii* and *suggestio falsi* can get them out of potentially dangerous circumstances, or can maliciously create difficulties for colleagues, or can project an image of themselves greater than the truth, and most of them carry this lesson over into the adult world.)

There is little to suggest that the purposes of writing are different in any way from those of speaking. The medium and convention being different, the chance given by writing to organise and control what is stated, the lack of immediate secondary factors such as obtain in spoken dialogue, might all result in a different form of expression, but the basic motivation is probably quite similar. According to Clark and Clark (3), the fundamental function of language is communication, and three elements are necessary, a speaker, a listener and a signalling system (a language).

These elements are the same in the writing convention, except that the substitution of 'writer' for speaker and 'reader' for listener would be required. Of course, there is nothing that says that a writer cannot write for himself alone. It is not absolutely necessary that there be a separate reader or readers. This question of a dialogue with the self takes one into a separate, though related, field, but will be discussed elsewhere in this chapter, in the section on 'thought and language.'

Basing their own commentary on Searle, the categories given by Clark and Clark (4) (pp 88-91) describe all (or most) speech acts (or by extension, writing acts as well), and their utilisation by a listener (or by extension, a reader). They are reproduced here for quick reference:

> Speech acts are limited in their variety. There are only some things people can do by uttering a sentence, and this is reflected in the limited purposes that can be imparted by their utterances. **George owns a car** usually has the force of an assertion, while **Does George own a car?** has the force of a request for information, and **I warn you that George owns a car,** the force of a warning. Each utterance is said to have a different kind of *illocutionary force*. Yet (according to Searle), every speech act falls into one of only five very general categories:
>
> (1) *Representatives.* The speaker, in uttering a representative, conveys his belief that some proposition is true. The representative *par excellence* is the assertion. When someone asserts **George owns a car,** he conveys his belief that the proposition **George owns a car** is true.
>
> (2) *Directives.* By uttering a directive, the speaker attempts to get the listener to do something. By ordering, commanding, requesting, begging, or pleading, the speaker is trying to get the listener to carry out some action. By asking a yes/no question like **Does** George **own a car?** or a WH-question like **What does George own?,** he is trying to get the listener to provide

information. Requests and questions are the two main types of directives.

(3) *Commissives.* By uttering a commissive, the speaker is committing himself to some future course of action. A prime example is the promise, but the category also includes vows, pledges, contracts, guarantees, and other types of commitments.

(4) *Expressives.* If the speaker wishes to express his "psychological state" about something, he utters an expressive. When he apologizes, thanks, congratulates, welcomes or deplores, he is expressing how good or bad he feels about some event and is therefore uttering an expressive.

(5) *Declarations.* When the speaker utters a declaration his very words bring about a new state of affairs. When he says **You're fired, I resign, I hereby sentence you to five years in prison,** or **I christen this ship H.M.S *Pinafore,*** he is declaring, and thereby causing your job to be terminated, his job to be terminated, you to spend five years in prison, or this ship to be named H.M.S *Pinafore.* Most declarations are specialized for use within a particular cultural system, such as employment, the church, law, or government.

Each of these categories requires something different of the listeners. Representatives require them to take note of the speaker's beliefs. Directives require them to determine some course of action and carry it out. Commissives, expressives, and declarations all require them to take note of new information: namely, the speaker's intended course of action, his feelings about some fact, or the change in formal status of some object (Note: something might be eluding the author here, but he is not sure into which category the *giving of permission* falls. Permission to do something is open-ended, leaving it to the will and volition of the recipient of the permission to do or not to do what has been permitted, so it is not commissive or directive. Nor does it seem to be expressive, declarative or representative)

If these categories are accepted as they stand, it cannot be seen that the illocutionary pressures of writing are different in any way. And, just as in speaking, the listener sometimes goes beyond the confines of these categories for the interpretation and utilisation of spoken utterances, so also must a reader sometimes 'read between the lines' for what the writer intended, or what the reader thinks he intended. The resolution of ambiguities is a part of the decoding process in reading, as it is in listening. What, after all, did Keats want his readers to understand when he wrote {*Ode on a Grecian Urn,* opening line):

'Thou still unravish'd bride of quietness'?

The ambiguity is, of course, in the word 'still'. It can mean 'quiet and unmoving'; or it can express surprise that something that should have happened has not yet happened. Had Keats inserted a comma he might have reduced some of the ambiguity. A lot would depend on the intonation put into reading it. As it stands it could be either the first adjective in a sequence of two, or an adverb modifying the adjective. Keats was writing in the nineteenth century, which is otherwise known for an irritating excess of commas. Nowadays there is a tendency to reduce them to the bare minimum, but this tendency can also be overdone.

The listener has many difficulties to contend with, mumbled words ('he *hurt* him' *vs* 'he *heard* him'), extraneous sounds (passing traffic, coughs, sneezes, other people talking, etc.), his own inattentiveness, the redundancies and false starts of speech ('ers', 'umphs', 'you sees' and 'I means'(fillers in general), repetitions, hesitation, self-correction, bad organisation, personality pressures (psychological interaction, dominance, subordination, preferences, dislikes), gestures and sloppy expression. He must do a fair amount of interpreting and guessing in order to understand what the speaker means, or wants him to do. Against this, the reader has a steady series of words printed on paper, to which he can refer several times if he is unsure of his interpretation.

By right, the written word should be less ambiguous than the spoken one. Of course, all language, spoken or written, is ambiguous. Speech has the advantage of gesture, stress and intonation to reduce if not eliminate ambiguity, whereas writing has the advantage of deliberative selection to get it as nearly right as the writer thinks possible, anticipating as much as he can the several traps into which the reader might fall, before it appears on paper.

Thought and Language

The natural progression in the production of language seems to be from thought to language. It is the progression adopted by Chomsky in his discussion on deep and surface structures. Some kind of ideation precedes expression, even at the deep level. This bubble of thought or feeling cannot be described in language, because it comes before language. It becomes aware of itself when it drapes itself in language, but the language might not be adequate for the purpose. It quickly makes for itself a lump of linguistic wood out of the 'language forest' resources at the user's disposal, rough hewn and uncertain at this point, but at least something linguistically tangible to work upon, much as a whittler looks for a suitable piece of wood and first shapes it to approximate dimensions before he tackles detail.

This basic shape in language can be described as the kernel utterance or sentence. There is no proof that such a process actually takes place, but the assumption is reasonable. One can see the whittler looking around for a suitable piece of wood and then cutting and carving it, but one cannot see the brain dipping into its own reserves, coming up with the beginnings of a linguistic utterance, and then working on that utterance to shape it suitably before presenting it.

What emerges as the final or surface utterance might be different from the kernel structure, but recognisably derived from it. Changes might take place in accordance with certain 'rules' of transformation (addition, deletion, substitution and re-ordering) until the writer is satisfied that the final product is ready to be offered to the world.

The basic idea might need to be re-ordered in the

form of a question, or re-worded to suit the mental level of a certain readership, or changed from the active to the passive voice, or from the simple to the continuous, or from direct to indirect speech to give continuity to what has gone before or what has been vaguely planned in totality. And, as it stands, the rough sentence may not be appropriate for the topic itself. A mature scholar might find his base words too 'hard' for the thing he is talking about, or for the level of his readership. Like using philosophical language for describing a cricket match to half-literate sports fans, or medico-legal terminology for giving a group of housewives instructions in how to carve a leg of mutton.

The difference between what happens in language and what the whittler does in the example given earlier, is of unconscious or conscious application. The criteria whereby the brain judges the appropriacy of a surface structure to its own topic and to its likely readership or audience, are applied unconsciously and with extreme rapidity. They form part of the speaker's total world-view, itself the product of his experience and understanding of the world at that point in life.

Within a given framework of culture, experience and background, appropriacy for one person should mean at least *near* appropriacy for another. However, commonality of culture and background does not eliminate individual differences of perception, so tensions, disagreements and confusions are to be expected despite the speaker's best efforts. Suffice it to say at this point, in the production of language the brain is unconsciously or subconsciously picking up guidelines and clues from its social surroundings, and judging a multitude of factors in reference to the topic of that language, to the world around it, and to the people in that world to whom the owner of that brain addresses that language. These are the moulds into which he pours the fluid elements of his productive linguistic resources. Eventually what he releases into the world in the form of an utterance in speech or writing, will be the product of his (usually) unconscious subjective judgement of a host of factors.

A simplified hypothetical model of what might happen in this process is offered below. It is emphasised here that this is all speculative. However, there must be some reason or reasons why, in a given context and situation, the brain prefers to use 'like' rather than 'eat' or 'consume' when it has several words in its lexical reservoir.

1. *Base thought*: John (singular)/ eat (habitual)/ fish

2. *Early inflectional correction of the verb to form the kernel sentence*:

   John eats fish

3. *Possible difficulties anticipated for the listener/reader:*
   a.   He might not know who John is

4. *First correction-- add information:*
   a.   my neighbour's son
   Second correction-- add more information:
   b. my neighbour's eldest son

5. *Possible verbs for use in the predicate*: like, love, eat, consume, devour, ingest, gobble, gulp, swallow, etc.

6. Selection determined unconsciously by levels of appropriacy; some too formal, some too informal, some indelicate, some which do not give the basic purpose of making the utterance, or the idea behind it:
    a. eat (OK, but rather blunt for a squeamish society)
    b. ingest (pretentious)
    c. love (too strong)
    d. like (all right)

7. *Possible expressions for the object noun:*
    a. fish
    b. sea-food
    c. fresh-water food
    d. white meat
    e. moving water creatures
    f. denizens of the deep
    g. finny aquatic creatures

9. Selection determined unconsciously by criteria of appropriacy: some of these expressions are pedantic or unnecessarily poetic, some are silly, and some obscure rather than reveal meaning. The occasion is not a poetry recital but a simple exchange between people chatting to

each other across a fence:
a. fish

10. The final product might be:

John, my neighbour's eldest son, likes fish.

11. Even as he finishes it, other thoughts might intrude. An element of doubt might trouble him even as the transformations take place. This could be solved by adding a tag at the end, as a quick, last fraction-of-a-second correction to introduce a little uncertainty:

John, my neighbour's eldest son, likes fish, doesn't he?

12. A stronger questioning mode could be adopted before releasing the utterance, in which case additions and re-ordering would be undertaken. If the primary purpose is to ask a question, the question transformations would be built into the utterance quite early, depending on whether it is (a) a 'yes/no' type of question which asks for a specific answer, or (b) a general WH-word type of question:
    a. John, my neighbour's eldest son, likes fish (?)[do] "Does John, my neighbour's eldest son, like fish?"

b. John, my neighbour's eldest son, likes fish (?) [what] "What does John, my neighbour's eldest son, like?"

Syntagmatic and paradigmatic choices are involved. The surface utterance might be very far indeed from the kernel utterance. Nevertheless, the basic idea remains visible through the transformations. Chomsky insists that transformations do not alter the core meaning of the base thought; 'John eats fish' means the same as 'fish is eaten by John'. However, some affirmatives cannot be passivised, and writers like Aitcheson (5) state that "Chomsky may be right in some respects, and wrong in others." Assertions like these need to be tested, but, because of the inaccesibility of the brain's functions it is doubtful if they will ever be confirmed.

In the foregoing examples, the progression is from the idea (undetectable until it uses a bit of language for itself) to the final expression. All appraisals, naive or sophisticated, of this progression, seem to confirm that it is mono-directional and proceeds in the manner described. The whittler cannot go from the finished product back to the lump of wood. However, as Aitcheson notes (6), it was as fashionable to follow Chomsky in the nineteen sixties as it was fashionable to oppose him in the nineteen seventies. The link between 'finished product' and 'lump of wood' in the analogy given here is, in any case, unsatisfactory, as whittling cannot be compared with something as commonplace yet as complex and elusive as human language.

It used to be said that only 'mad' people talked to themselves, but the phenomenon is universal. The interesting part of this phenomenon is not that people talk to themselves but why they do so. If language is all or nearly all produced in the unconscious, surely it knows what it is thinking. The individual might need to verbalise his ideas for others, but why bother to do it for himself? Surely the kernel utterance or even its predecessor, the un-verbalised thought, should be enough since the person knows what he wants and what the idea stands for, without bothering to process it until it reaches a surface form. Yet people do process language fully, even for themselves. They also write to themselves. They keep notes of their own thoughts. They relate experiences in personal diaries. They write things down for themselves, so that they can make decisions about them or solve problems. In fact, some inner processes would be very difficult to organise without this self-externalising ability, even though what is written down goes no farther than a quick perusal before it reaches the wastepaper basket. Doing sums is certainly easier on paper than in the head. This phenomenon places some of the assumptions of transformation in doubt. In telling himself something, a person often feels the need of a fully structured internal, or externalised, utterance in preference to an amorphous bubble of thinking.

There is a simultaneity about thought and language which makes it extremely difficult to assert that either precedes the other. Since one cannot detect the existence of a pre-verbalised thought until it begins to verbalise itself, it is tempting to claim that what is observed as the language *is, in fact,* the thought; in which case every transformation is not a transformation or change, it *is a new expression of a new idea.* Judged in this way, what one thinks of as a transformation is not merely another version of a roughly conceived base structure, derived by the application of one or some of a limited number of possibilities to the original idea, it is the linguistic manifestation of its own thought.

This is a proper 'chicken-and-egg' argument, and, as it stands, there is no way of settling it. Thought simultaneously generates language, and language simultaneously generates thought. If this perception is accepted, then all surface structures represent their own related thoughts. The argument about deep and surface structures, and the progression of transformations from deep to surface utterances cannot be demonstrated, although there is an instinctive feeling about its rightness on most points. But then, nothing of what goes on in the brain can ever be settled. We have Libet's experimentally validated observation that mental activity precedes awareness (mentioned in Chapter One) which would lead one to believe that thought (unconscious mental activity) precedes language (verbalized consciousness), and this is how it stands at this stage, at least for this author.

There are probably some elements of unobtrusive verbalisation even when a person seems to be thinking in pictures or sounds, as a painter or musician might. But there cannot be much verbalisation when a man driving a car suddenly stamps on the brake pedal and wrenches his vehicle sideways to prevent an accident. Nevertheless some kind of reflex 'thinking' must have taken place, if the job was done properly. Likewise, a good tennis player 'knows' his opponent is about to place the ball down the line, without telling himself so in explicit language. He does not then instruct himself to move quickly forward and slide to the left, in order to intercept it. He just does it. A person's habit and reflex systems can act very rapidly in apparently 'thought out' patterns and without any conscious verbalisation at the time.

However, underscoring this argument is the popular definition of thinking. Thinking might not be confined to the brain and might take place in rudimentary, repetitive, reflexive ways in other parts of the body, especially the muscles. But this connotation of the word is not common. After the near-accident, the driver of the car mentioned in the example given earlier might explain to the policeman that he acted 'without thinking', underscoring a popular belief that *real* thinking is what is done in language. This adds to the difficulties encountered here, because it turns the argument back into itself—if there is no language, there is no thinking; and if there is no thinking, there is no language. It is *point-zero* in the discussion.

Is this relevant? It might be so, if there is any degree of truth in the hypothesis that thought is as much a product of language as language is of thought, and that improving one improves the other, much as stronger bones go side-by-side with stronger muscles. It is the basis of much that happened in writing theory with regard to sentence combining and language manipulation in the nineteen seventies and eighties, which still has adherents today, that learning how to use his language in a mature, flexible way, helps the learner to think in mature, flexible patterns.

In the same way as directly exercising and strengthening the muscles leads indirectly but simultaneously to stronger bones, so directly exercising and strengthening the ability to write leads indirectly but simultaneously to stronger thinking powers. If the purpose is to strengthen the bones, this has to be done indirectly, through the muscles. If the idea is to improve the functioning of the brain, this might possibly be done indirectly, through writing.

The attractive part of this hypothesis is that if the purpose is to improve thinking, this can be realised indirectly, through language, especially writing. There is little doubt that the tool can affect performance. A sharp knife that sits easily in the hand, will not only allow the whittler to do what he wants better than a blunt one; it might even create possibilities for him that he had not thought of before. People who play games such as tennis, know how much a well-strung, properly balanced racquet can affect their game. If it seems right for them, they will probably succeed in playing strokes they never imagined existed in their repertoire before. So also, the possession of well-honed linguistic skills might create opportunities of thinking and expression he did not have before.

The researcher has repeatedly mentioned writing rather than speaking as the primary tool in this process. Speaking might make a 'ready' man in the Baconian sense, a man able to think on his feet in quick but probably limited patterns of language. Verbally 'fluent' people probably use a smaller but more readily available and oft-repeated vocabulary than hesitant speakers who grope their way through a large but less readily retrievable storehouse of words. Writing has the advantage over speaking here because it is all down on paper. The learner can see what he is doing and can experiment with it, or change or manipulate it as required, while the possession of a large vocabulary does not hinder fluency in this medium, as it might do in speaking.

These matters will be taken up in greater detail in the chapter on writing and its role in mental development.

Chapter 5 Notes

1. Britton, J., *Language and Learning,* Penguin, 1970, 174

2. Halliday, M, *Explorations in the Functions of Language,* Edwin Arnold., 1973, 17-18

3. Clark and Clark, 24-25

4. Ibid., 88-89 [Searle, J., ^CA Taxonomy of Illocutionary Acts", *University of Minnesota Stuies on the Philosophy of Language,* University of Minnesota Press, 1975]

5. Aitcheson, *The Articulate Mammal,* 108

6. Ibid., 20

Chapter Six
The Process of Writing

Some models of probable factors in the production of language were suggested in the previous chapter. The argument so far has treated writing in isolation, but, of course, forming a *gestalt* of a word in its wholeness is clearly facilitated by frequent and wide reading. After some practice, the eye and brain can learn to see words, and even phrases, sentences or discourse segments, as wholes, thus greatly facilitating the speed and efficiency of the reading process. In fact reading can proceed at great velocity as the brain sorts out the useful from the redundant in what the eye peruses, adding things, skipping over things, ignoring things, interpreting things, agreeing or disagreeing with things. The brain is a naturally rapid processor, doing what it does half-consciously or quite unconsciously at enormous speeds.

Of the literacy' skills, it is this perception of wholeness that makes reading more natural than writing, while the 'oracy' skills are natural by definition. The speaker conceives of words and utterances as wholes. For example, he will automatically use a plural form of the verb for a plural noun, and within the limits of his concurrent memory to 'glue[5] what he wants to say together, can look anaphorically behind to what he has said already and cataphorically forward to what he intends to say, in order to organise his discourse into fairly large segments. In trying to decipher what he hears, the good listener uses complementary mental tools and conceptions at great speed, so that he not only keeps up with another person's speech, he sometimes anticipates and completes it before he has heard it.

This is not true of writing. Whether by hand or by machines such as typewriters or computers, it is basically a slow process of assembling things from parts to wholes. The physical constraints on writing make it tardy, so that it is often far in arrears of what the brain is trying to think and say. For example, what is written on this page has taken several minutes. A good reader could scan and extract what he wanted from it in a few seconds.

At the same time it must be said that it is precisely because of this kind of delay in writing that one gets a chance to improve a misapplication; such as this author's tendency to displace the limiter 'only' ('she *only* invited the women to her party' when what he wants to say is 'she invited *only* the women to her party') in speech. This is less likely to happen in writing.

The brain seems to be forced to move at somewhat the same tempo as the medium it is using for expression. In speaking the movement is faster. People with good, flexible vocal cords can speak very rapidly indeed, and this allows the brain to think rapidly, except that, as noted before, the thinking patterns and vocabulary of speaking tend to be limited.

Except for people using phonetic shorthand systems, writing, no matter how good, is comparatively slow. The brain has to adjust accordingly, though the adjustment might not always be in perfect harmony with the medium.

Compared with the other skills, from the standpoint of *gestalt* theory writing is the wrong way of using the brain for communication; the brain is leaping all over the place with fragments of ideas or even whole ideas while the hand is still wavering over spelling, words, syntax and punctuation. There is a lack of synchronicity between thought and expression. As the least natural of the communicative skills, writing is therefore the one that needs the most care. However, the premise of this chapter is that the act of writing grooves the brain into some kind of parallel activity, even with regard to speed.

Only one productional difficulty will be mentioned here before proceeding with an analysis of factors in writing. It stems from the Anglicised version of the alphabet. Problems with spelling have been mentioned before, in chapters one and three. With the development of the alphabet from its beginnings in the Middle East and its movement to Europe for adaptation to European languages, what started out as an arbitrary and fairly simple process of matching and associating symbol to sound has become, over the centuries, a complex business of capital letters, punctuation marks, spelling and construction.

Some languages bracket a question with two question marks, one straight and the other upside down. Others have diacritical marks to indicate variations. Some are festooned with them in an attempt to capture the real sounds of the language on paper, little loops, wavy lines, dots, heads, tails or oblique dashes adorning the basic letters all over the place.

English uses only one question mark, and is free of diacritics (the dot over the small 'i' and the cross on the 't' are part of the shape of those letters) except when it uses incompletely indigenized imports like 'naivete' or 'sturm'. It has learnt to make do with twenty six letters for most of its phonological needs, despite a great deal of imbalance between traditional symbol and sound. This 'reduction' to basic letters is both good and bad, good because it employs an alphabet less 'cluttered' than some others and, therefore, easier to learn in its essentials, bad because that alphabet falls short of the phonological needs of the language. Between the good and the bad, the foreign learner has to adapt to spelling and presentational norms as judged correct by native speakers.

This is not an easy task. Nor is it an entirely settled task. Should such a learner use 'centre' or 'center', 'instil' or 'instill', 'enrollment' or 'enrolment'? He sees both forms in the world today. Why should 'travelled' be spelt with a double 'l' by the British when the stress is not on the preceding syllable, which seems to be the rule governing the double 'r' in words like 'referred'? And what about the word 'spelt' itself? Should it be 'spelled'? Till the early part of the twentieth century words like 'dropped' and 'stepped' were found quite commonly spelt with a 'pt' ending instead of the 'pped' ending we find almost universally today. The 'ed' ending seems to be replacing the older 't' ending in words like 'learnt', and 'spelt' (with a double 'l'). The word 'dreamt' is occasionally seen as 'dreamed' and 'lit' as 'lighted'. But 'slept' has shown no sign of changing to 'sleeped'. In the researcher's childhood 'learned' (pronounced with the last syllable sounded) was used as an adjective to describe a scholarly person, and 'learnt' for the past tense or past participle. Looking for common patterns is likely to fail, and the cry of 'the exception proves the rule' is misleading. The exception proves little more than the exception. Sometimes the run of exceptions, and of exceptions within those exceptions, simply swamps the rules. Most cases and exceptions have to be learnt as separate items. This imposes a heavy burden on the foreign writer.

Anomalies abound. Efforts at standardisation have been made for centuries. Caxton's early efforts with printing helped, together with the productions of major lexicographers such as Johnson and Webster, but agreement is far from final even today. The following examples have been taken from two different editions of *The Canterbury Tales* by Chaucer:

1. That had a fire-red cherubinnes face—
   For saucefleem he was, with eyen narrwe:

   (Penguin)

2. That hadde a fyr-reed cherubinnes face,
   For sawcefleem he was, with eyen narwe

   (ed., Coghill, N)

Other versions exist as well. They serve to show how much writing once depended on the preferences and whims of early scribes. As with other aspects of language, spelling has undergone and is still undergoing change.

In Pakistan no assumptions can be made for many students reaching advanced levels. Productional difficulties will be encountered in spelling, paragraphing, punctuation and overall planning. Ideas for improving them are given in chapter nine.

Basic factors

Marzano mid DiStefano (1) identify the following factors:

1. Motivation
2. Topic identification
3. Audience identification
4. Identification of format
5. Collection of information
6. Putting thoughts to paper
7. Polishing

The researcher prefers the words 'reader' for 'audience', since no element of hearing or listening is involved. Of interest is that 'putting thoughts to paper' actually comes sixth on the list, and that a lot of preparatory judging, collecting and thinking (what the authors describe as 'pre-writing') is deemed to be desirable before the writer commits himself.

According to these authors:

> All seven steps are integral parts of writing, although, some tasks are more important than others in different writing situations. For example, in formal writing

polishing is probably the most critical....and most writing done in connection with college courses is formal...we have devoted more chapters to polishing than to any other phase of writing (2)

Motivation

Motivation precedes everything else, and as stated earlier, may be instrinsic or extrinsic, the first kind generally being considered better than the second. That which springs from within is likely to be closer to the heart and mind of the user of the language and to lead to a more interesting and expressive kind of writing. That which comes from without, usually in the form of an assignment to be tendered to a certain tutor within a certain time-frame, is likely to be constrained by what the student thinks his tutor wants him to do, and by the limitations of the time-frame itself. Also, there may be rigid or strongly recommended requirements of format and presentation, all likely to inhibit basic creativity. After all, creativity is by definition the exploration of uncharted ways, and this is unlikely when there is a firm insistence on following well-charted academic grooves. Nevertheless, this is the most common source of motivation for the student. He has tutors and examiners to satisfy.

Externally derived motivation is less effective when it is couched in the didactic mode, and more effective when it is offered as a goal-oriented appeal to the imagination rather than to the analytical functions of the brain. In the field of practical psychology called *cybernetics,* goals given to the subconscious mind as mental images have the power to 'motivate' the individual and, more significantly, to point the way to the achievement of those goals. This can be done by the individual for himself:

> I have found, for example, that if 1 have to write upon some rather difficult topic, the best plan is to think about it with great intensity— the greatest intensity of which I am capable— for a few hours or days, and at the end of that time give orders, so to speak, that the work is to proceed underground... .Before I discovered this technique I used to spend (a lot of time) worrying because I was making no progress...
> (3)

The first step, then, is motivation. But this would not consist of simple exhortations to do something coupled with a personal fear that it might not be done properly, nor would it proceed at all satisfactorily from threats given by the teacher or the system. That motivation is best that generates movement towards the desired goal and also shows the way towards its successful completion.

Marzano and DiStefano summarise it as follows:

> ...we can say that the cybernetic theory of motivation is based on four tenets:
>
> (1) All people possess a goal-seeking cybernetic mechanism sometimes referred to as the subconscious mind
>
> (2) The subconscious mind will automatically motivate us to accomplish the goals that are given to it by the conscious mind

(3) One of the major ways the conscious mind gives goals to the subconscious mind is by the use of mental images

(4) Once goals are given to the subconscious mind, an attempt should be made to stop conscious mind thoughts that are contrary to those goals (4)

In dealing with motivation, the teacher can safely assume that there is a lot of negative thinking among students with regard to writing of all kinds, but especially of externally determined essays and assignments. His primary job is to assure them that they *can* induce themselves to want to write *and* that they *can* be successful at writing.

His procedures in doing so will revolve around some kind of cybernetic applications, but without saying so overtly. Some of the teacher's art, like that of the poet, is best when it conceals itself. In the first phase, he has to show his students how to activate *internal* mechanisms, how to motivate *themselves* to do something derived from the outside world. This would consist of envisioning for themselves the successful completion of the piece of work, giving themselves reasonable dead-lines (unreasonable ones are self-defeating) and generating an atmosphere of successful achievement and self-approval for their own efforts. However, all this can be crushed by an insensitive, negativistic, hypercritical teacher. So, on the other hand, the second phase of motivation requires that the teacher provide an *external* framework of positive reinforcements in the form of encouragement, approval and praise.

The impulse to write can come from inner needs also,

and these are more likely to prompt the writer into doing something than those derived from outside. However, many writers inhibit themselves here as well, because it is in the nature of writing that it may be exposed to the eyes of others, and there is always the fear of failure and ridicule. Whether the motivation is inner or outer, the product might ultimately be in the possession of the world at large, and there are some people so sensitive about rejection or disapproval that they prefer not to do anything at all.

Referring back to chapter four, one sees that writing need not be made available to others for critical evaluation. Shy people can write under pseudonyms if they intend what they write to be read by others. Alternatively, if they are so overwhelmed by the possibility of ridicule they can simply keep their writings to themselves.

However, these last two options are not available to students, since they live under the repeated glare of testing and evaluation. In general it may be stated that the goals of externally derived motivation are fairly clearly defined by the teacher, system, academic programme or market place, while those of internally derived motivation tend to be diffuse and personal. Either way, inner or outer, a person's chief resource is himself. A young person in his early twenties already has a large fund of experience to dip into, and a well-developed brain able to retrieve, comprehend, compare, analyse, judge and accept or reject data supplied from wherever it comes, without and within. His first tool is the brain itself.

Topic Identification

A student does not usually have much control over topic

selection or identification. He might be given some choice, but most topics will be supplied by his teacher. Occasionally he might want to contribute something of his own to a college newsletter or departmental magazine. Very rarely, he might be asked to write a few pages on a topic of his own choice.

It was stated above that the ordinary young adult has already acquired a lot of knowledge about the world, and that he could probably find a lot to write about from his own experience. He could also derive sensible comments from that same fund of experience about almost anything given to him to write about. The brain is an astounding storehouse of impressions. Wayne Dyer says:

> ...the brain, which is composed of perhaps ten billion working parts has enough storage capacity to accept ten new facts every second. It has been conservatively estimated that the human brain can store an amount of information equivalent to one hundred trillion words, and that all of us use but a tiny fraction of this storage space.. .(5)

People complain that the right answer to a puzzle, or the right retort to somebody else's rudeness, often comes too long after the event to do much good. This is because of the subconscious mechanisms mentioned earlier, which work in their own mysterious ways in accordance with their own rhythms. The brain has a good retrieval system, but it is not always a ready one, especially under the press and tension of examinations. Marazon and DiStefano suggest the technique of 'free-writing' to stimulate the flow of ideas from within. Whatever comes into the mind should be noted down for a few minutes, even if it seems all disjointed and irrelevant in the beginning:

> .. .the basic idea behind free-writing is to allow your pen, pencil or typewriter to record your thoughts as quickly as possible without attending to grammar, spelling or punctuation. You shouldn't even try to write in complete sentences. What you put down on paper should be a representation of the random thoughts running through your mind...(6)

The authors cited above go on to explain that free writing can be unstructured or structured. Unstructured free writing applies no restrictions whatsoever, and the result can be half a page starting out in many directions, with some directions apparently more developed than others, strung loosely together without a recognisable sequence in a barely legible scrawl, with no capital letters or punctuation. Out of such a disordered mass a person might find several things to write about.

Structured free writing is not quite as free as this, as it might focus on some remembered event, or some sensory feeling, or on some personal opinion about such an event or feeling. The difference is that there is a guiding element in structured free writing that is lacking in unstructured free writing. However, all approaches to this kind of writing will ignore constraints of form or presentation. As a topic generating technique, it focuses on ideas rather than on form.

A step further in reducing the time lag between thinking and writing mentioned earlier is 'brain storming', a free play of associations recorded in words rather than in finished or half-finished utterances, so that the momentum of ideas is not lost in language. Both free writing and brain storming are attempts to bring the slow march of writing more in line with the quick, grasshopper jumps of the brain. Brain storming is not always an individual effort, and can be employed by a small group of people tossing ideas around from one to the other until some general pattern or agreement becomes visible.

Topics to write about can also be found in the world around one. Somebody' else's experience, or opinion, or observation, can become a starting point, or a film or TV programme might result in a train of thought. Books are a fertile source of topics and for the student will probably be the main source for at least the duration of their studentship, apart from the topics they are given to write about in examination papers and regular assignments.

Reader Profile

Three factors dominate in the determination of level, register and style. The first is the purpose of the author in writing what he writes (this might also take into account the purpose of the reader in reading it)—it might be to inform, persuade or entertain, or simply help the reader with his own purpose; the second his topic; and the third a profile of his reader, if he can make one successfully. The last factor is important, but once a piece of writing is given to the world, it is difficult to say who might or might not read it. This is not a great problem for the student, who knows that his offerings will go mainly to his teachers or examiners. It can be a problem for someone who publishes his writing. Even so, a writer usually has some reader or category of readers in mind when he writes—old Sourface the teacher, for example, who keeps talking about brevity and relevance; or children between 6 and 8; or amateur home-gardeners—and the way he sets about writing his piece will be affected by that category.

If he is a specialist writing for specialists, there will be one set of assumptions, and another for a specialist writing for laymen. If he is a layman writing for specialists there will be yet another, and yet one more for a layman writing for laymen. Subtle signals come into the equation when there are age, group, sex or ethnic differences. The writer has to be specially careful not to hurt feelings on touchy issues, and might have to use 'politically correct' or 'gender sensitive' language, which could entail a lot of re-writing and revision. For example, for linguistic convenience, the author has used the pronoun 'he' to include 'she' in this thesis, although he is aware of the fact that at all levels there are more women than men in teaching, and about as many women students as men at higher levels of study. This could be misconstrued as typical male insensitivity.

Specific areas also exist. Writing may need to be done in special categories, like 'medical report writing' or 'business communication'. A degree of facility with specialist jargon and a knowledge of format and presentation would be expected in such fields. Within the generally poor acquisition of writing skills in English in Pakistan and the time constraints experienced at higher levels, the answer might be to focus not on English in general but on the kind of English a student might encounter in his chosen field, thus giving him a linguistic survival packet likely to be useful in his professional life. Does a medical student, for example, need to know anything about 'hamartia' or the 'iambic pentameter'? Does a student teacher of geography need to know what 'mucocutaneous leishmaniasis' means?

It is nice if everybody could learn everything about everything, but there is not enough time, especially at the student level, so pragmatic selections are indicated. The idea *of English for Specific Purposes* arises from such a range of practical needs, that there be well-planned, properly delimited and suitably structured language courses for intending physicists, chemists, engineers, doctors, businessmen and so on. For example, scientific English uses the passive voice quite a lot—'John heated the water' introduces an irrelevant agent, whereas 'the water was heated', as it would be in scientific writing, removes the agent. The advantages of this approach are, first, that students have a defined quantity of language to function within, and, second, that their writings will be assessed in terms of that definition and not in terms of some other assumption.

Arguments can be found against this approach. Specific English might not be very different from 'general' English, and a specialist vocabulary is soon acquired if the base is already strong. It is probably true that a student who already has a good general grasp of English can move fairly easily into specialist fields, but that a student who has learnt only one kind of English to draw upon might feel handicapped in the general world. The general can quickly absorb the specific, but the specific cannot grow so easily into the general. Also, is it possible to talk about the language of physics, say, without taking extensive excursions into physics itself? If the focus is on language rather than knowledge, examples and illustrations taken from the subject will tend to be simplified and trivialised. If the examples and illustrations are presented in a form as complex as they are found in the subject, then the focus will no longer be on the language of physics but on physics itself. But that is not the purpose of the specific language course.

Objections notwithstanding, specific courses do seem to help students in their transition to professional studies, and some specificity of purpose and recognition of reader-characteristics do help the writer. Among this author's comments in chapter ten is a recommendation that students be given such interstitial courses, especially in writing, at all stages, to induct them into the kind of language they are likely to encounter a few months or weeks later. A great deal more activity than what happens in the country today, in the mounting of special courses and in the directed, purposeful teaching of English, is indicated.

It helps the writing process if all three factors are identified and described. Some writers do it in elaborate outlines on paper. Many writers do it in considerable detail mentally. In a haphazard, unplanned manner, all writers do it to some degree. The advantage *of* conscious planning shows up later in the actual writing, which tends to be focused and well-organised rather than meandering and formless.

Format

There is a general sense in which writing is imaged on paper. Some students have a better 'visual intelligence' than others, and organise their writing so that thoughts follow one another in a comprehensible sequence, either chronologically or logically. The question of format is simply in line with the idea that the writer should show good manners towards his readers, make what he is trying to say easy for them to understand, pleasing to the eye and patterned in a way likely to help them. We find recommendations such as the seven 'C's:

> ...To compose effective written...messages, you must apply certain communication principles. These principles provide guidelines for choice of content and style of presentation, adapted to the purpose and receiver of your message. Called the "seven C's" they are completeness, conciseness, consideration, concreteness, clarity, courtesy, and correctness... (7)

These authors state that the origin of the "seven C's" formula is obscure (8), but that good writing from Greek times exhibits conscious or unconscious application of the formula.

Each "C" category has its own components. 'Completeness' would entail providing all necessary information and answering all questions, 'conciseness' would eliminate wordiness, avoid repetition and include only relevant material, 'consideration' would focus on the receiver rather than on the sender and would emphasize the positive over the negative, 'concreteness' would insist on demonstrable fact and incorporate the use of action words and concrete images, 'clarity' would adopt a selection of language suitable for the total purpose of the writing, 'courtesy' would employ appropriate tones and graces, and 'correctness' would maintain adequate control over both fact and language (9).

Writing in English has developed its own sense of rightness over the centuries. It tends to proceed in a linear fashion. There is usually a *beginning* in the sense of a quick introduction, a *middle* in which the main mass of information is presented, and an *end* which summarises or concludes the piece. English writing has a strong sense *of paragraph,* a grouping of related ideas which helps to divide the matter into readily comprehensible units of thought and language. Paragraphs themselves are organised round one central idea, often presented in what is called a *topic sentence.* The other statements in the paragraph illustrate, simplify or amplify that central idea. In all, English writing tends to be more fully organised than that of some other languages, These matters will be taken up later.

Collecting Information

It was mentioned earlier that the writer's chief resource is himself, and that he can usually find quite a lot to say about most things of common interest without needing to collect data. This is true even when he searches for facts from sources outside himself, because a lot will depend on the way he processes those facts. There are lots of things people know very little about. All public writing and reporting should be responsible and reliable, though there is often a big gap between the 'is' and the 'should be',

Academic writing in particular calls for a certain precision of statement coupled with a continuous and rigorous process of self-appraisal, and is expected to rest heavily on fact. The kind of facts a student would need are those garnered from libraries and books, though they may also come directly from teachers and colleagues, or from data collected as a result of an experiment.

The first stop in the journey is the reference book, and the main reference book is the dictionary. A good dictionary gives more than just meanings and spellings. Sources and origins might also be mentioned, and directions to other sources might also be given to consult for more details. Some large dictionaries are more like encyclopaedias in the way essential knowledge is given about key interests. Dictionaries can be general, or they can refer to special subjects or areas of study, such as medical terminology, music or economics.

Encyclopaedias are invaluable, and are organised alphabetically like dictionaries. Latest editions of the really large ones give just about everything required for a preliminary investigation into a chosen field. Some of them have been put on computers, making them readily available in the home and easy to use. As with dictionaries, specific-area encyclopaedias will also be found.

Almanacs and yearbooks give a continual updating of facts and events, and can provide a lot of useful information with contemporary relevance. They are often organised chronologically rather than alphabetically.

Atlases contain a lot of facts and figures about the physical world, and are sometimes joined with history, showing changing boundaries of nations over given spans of time, or with medicine, showing centres of infections or the spread of epidemics, or with other fields of knowledge, suggesting that there are no strictly defined demarcations in knowledge.

Other than reference books, good libraries offer detailed information through books, magazines and pamphlets about specific study areas in a variety of subjects. Some libraries are general. Others are weighted towards the kind of institution they serve: and, of course, one would not look for material on mediaeval allegorical literature in a science library.

Chapter 6 Notes

1. Marzano, R., and DiStefano, P., The Writing Process, D.Van Nostrand Company, NY, 1981, 7-8

2. Ibid., 8

3. Ibid., 13

4. Ibid., 14

5. Ibid., 25

6. Ibid., 26

7. Murhpy, H., Hildebrandt, H., and Thomas, J., *Effective Business Communication*, McGraw-Hill, NY., 1997, 32

8. Ibid., ix

9. Ibid., 32-64

Chapter Seven
Writing and its Role in Mental Development

Reciprocity

If mental development is understood to mean an increase in intelligence, the proposition will probably have to be rejected outright. It is fair, however, to point out that some of the early research conducted on the poor relative performance of disadvantaged minority communities in America indicated that learning good writing practices acted as a stimulant for intelligence as well (1). It is fair, also, to point out the inadmissibility of such studies--that one set of studies will be neutralised or contradicted by another seems to be one of the constants of linguistic, sociological and anthropological research (2). There might be many reasons for this. One suspects an element of bias and prejudgement in some cases, despite all the paraphernalia of objective controls. One suspects that the human subjects of these studies sometimes simply outthink the researchers. One suspects that human beings are simply too complex to be slotted into categories, a requirement so basic to the scientific method.

In the nineteen fifties and sixties, attempts were made to understand this phenomenon. Blacks and Chicanos brought into the mainstream of education tended to fall behind in academic output in comparison with relatively advantaged whites. It could not be seen as a matter of native intelligence without introducing the implications of racism. It was thought that it might be a question of language. The blacks had their own version of English, complete and fully comprehensible among themselves, but different in many points of vocabulary and structure, from that of the white majority. However, this could be fitted in somewhere as yet another dialect of English. It might occasion hilarity or bewilderment in some situations, but it was sufficiently comprehensible for ordinary interaction. Where there was a visible lag was in the field of literacy and writing.

A nexus between literacy and brain performance was postulated. Listening and speaking were put in a different linguistic convention from reading and writing. Some of the differences are obvious. Oracy is from the ear to the mouth, literacy is from the eye to the hand. The media are different, the channels are different, the operative assumptions are different, although both functions are controlled by the brain.

Natural intelligence seems to be an endowment decided by genes donated by parents paired with the efficient internal coordination of the brain's activities for the control of the organism itself, and for the comprehension of the environment. The genetic endowment might be high, but if the internal efficiency is damaged or disregarded in any way, which is quite possible in the uncertainties and hazards of living, it might or might not remain a fixed or nearly fixed quantity. There is a large area left to chance, to the accident of wealth or poverty, to the expectations of the individual's immediate environment, to opportunities presented by society. Very little is really known about the brain, although there is a lot of speculation about it. Early attempts to measure intelligence, though popular at one time, proved disappointing. The operative cultural and linguistic biases of the tests themselves were such as to raise doubts as to the validity of results drawn from them.

No teacher will deny that some students act with more aplomb and precision than others. Whether this is because of intelligence, interest or commitment is difficult to say. It may just be the result of a greater desire to cooperate, or, simply, of a greater interest in the subject. Some of the most bored and uncooperative of students are found to be highly 'intelligent' in fields that really do interest them. Many parts of formal education are tedious. It takes an effort of will on the part of students to plough their way through them.

As with learning, so with intelligence itself. The motivated mind stores certain facts and thinks about them in an intelligent way, while the disinterested mind tends to ignore them and thus seem 'unintelligent'. All teachers know of intractably dull students with whom hardly anything seems to register in the classroom, who can cite cricket scores in important matches since the known beginnings of the game, or discuss this or that bowler's merits with great animation and in impressive detail.

Although people think they know what it is, intelligence is not easily definable, and may not be quantifiable at all. It is a bit meaningless to talk about the implicit capacity of ten billion working parts. The possibilities are overpowering. Yet people regularly use quantifying terms for it, like 'my friend is *more* intelligent than I am'. It is pointed out with numbing frequency that all people use a very small percentage of their potential endowment, even the most intelligent of them. It is suggested that even morons and idiots have a huge potential of intelligence, and that a more accurate picture of the phenomenon is to think of it as nearly infinite in potential capacity, but used with variable efficiency by different people. Mr. A uses his brain more efficiently in some situations than Mr. B. This does not show that Mr. A is more intelligent than Mr. B; it merely shows a superior application of the brain in certain circumstances. The emphasis here is on application and usage, not on capacity. All people, Mr. A and Mr. B (and indeed Mr. C, the village idiot) are possessors of unimaginable reserves of intelligence.

Among other archeological and anthropological speculations, those who ascribe to evolutionary theories suggest that man's peculiar intelligence is the *product* of certain human activities and abilities not duplicated in animals. Human diet, for example, has been variegated throughout history, and the variety of food substances derived from different sources may have contributed to man's subtle and complex mental powers. It is also suggested that the thumb's ability to act opposite the lingers, enabling the human "paw' to grip and manipulate things in a variety of ways with infinite gradations of strength and pressure, would have demanded the controlling power of a large and complex brain behind it, thus stimulating brain growth in early man. Also, the peculiarly human phenomenon of the larynx dropping over the opening of the trachea about three to five months after birth, enabling humans to use their voices in a flexible way, would have had a key role in developing human intelligence, not so much in quantity, which is huge in any case, but in type.

Whether the opposed thumb came first or the descended larynx, is difficult to say. It is likely that the thumb came first, and that when the dropped larynx became a permanent feature of the species, it found a satisfactorily large brain already present and operating inside the organism, all ready for yet further growth and the development of language.

It is not a case of broad intelligence. Of interest is evidence to support the existence of a human sub-species with tool-making, artistic and community skills called Neanderthal Man *{Homo sapiens neanderthalensis)*, who lived from about 150,000 to about 30,000 years ago across parts of the Middle East and Europe, and then disappeared. Earlier speculation tended towards the belief that he was absorbed into the mainstream of the human species and therefore ceased to exist as a separate entity. It was said that modern people with the rhesus factor in their blood (positive blood types) had *neanderthalensis* in their lineage, and people without it (negative blood types) were essentially Cro-Magnon in ancestry. It is possible, however, that *neanderthalensis* represented a relatively non-productive branch in the evolution of the species and simply died out. Alternatively, he might have been driven off the earth by a more articulate, more *practically* intelligent, if not more *potentially* intelligent, branch of the same species (3). Bryson talks about Cro-Magnons 'outclassing' Neanderthals. There are instances of one set of human beings terminating another, as Spanish invaders did in parts of America, or British settlers did in Tasmania. However, this happened in confined areas in relatively modern times, and because of decisive technological advantages. It is difficult to picture pre-historic Cro-Magnons successfully eliminating all Neanderthals across a broad sweep of land from Iraq on one side, to Germany on the other.

From measurements it is determined that Neanderthal Man had a larger average brain (and therefore more potential intelligence, though perhaps of a different type) than that of modern man. From general skull and skeletal settings, it is deduced that he did not have a dropped larynx, and, therefore, was not able to develop language in the way humans can now, though he probably had enough communicative ability for collective hunting and for the essentials of corporate living.

This seems to have handicapped him in competition with Cro-Magnon Man *{Homo sapiens sapiens),* who turned up from Africa as the glaciers receded from parts of Europe at the end of the last ice-age, and laid claim to the same territories. With his somewhat smaller brain, but with the crucial physical characteristic of a descended larynx, Cro-Magnon is the direct ancestor of modem man. He had fully developed speech organs, which gave him decisive advantages in the competition for survival.

This would suggest that developed language abilities confer a survival advantage on a species over those with undeveloped (animals in general) or underdeveloped (*neanderthalensis,* for example) language abilities, regardless of brain size. It would also suggest that the physical ability to produce language results in a peculiarly human quality (not quantity, though perhaps some of that as well) of intelligence. It would confirm the nexus between language and thought mentioned in an earlier chapter, which seems to be an exclusively human monopoly. Above all, for the question of writing skills, it would strongly support the premise that improving writing skills might help to develop mental abilities.

The argument proceeds from the physical to the mental, from the developmental growth generated in the brain by the opposed thumb, to the special kind of intelligence generated by an ability to speak—fortuitous happenings in the evolution of the species. Why the larynx dropped cannot be determined, but the habitually upright posture of human beings might have had something to do with it. Apes and bears can also stand upright, but do so only when they must. One chance mutation which persists across generations to become a permanent characteristic, causes other changes in the dependent linkages of the organism. Man's erect posture, his front-seeing eyes (which he shares with apes and monkeys), his tool-making thumb (apes and monkeys have this also, but not in the same way) and his dropped larynx (which is exclusively human) are what made him into what he is now.

A lot of people might see the cart before the horse in these arguments. They would not be able to comprehend, for example, why the need for a certain amount of brain control generated by a subtle hand mechanism should have produced such a vast *excess* of brain capacity. If it is true that generations upon generations of human beings have never fully, or even significantly, used their brain capacity, why has that excess capacity not atrophied and withered away? Why did the organism waste evolutionary energy and time generating something it never used, never needed to use and never tried to use? They would say that the concept of a separate human species, designed *ab initio* and created by God as it is, with a big brain, an opposing thumb and an innate ability for language, has the unarguable sanction of faith and makes more sense than the assumption that one species might have grown out of another. Whatever the truth of either vision, what emerges is an exceedingly complex human organism with astounding abilities in thinking and communication and a brain reserve capacity of near infinite dimensions.

One observes a similar tendency to decry the Sapir-Whorf hypothesis, which also seems to go the 'wrong' way:

The Sapir-Whorf hypothesis:

In most cause-and-effect tandems, it is easy to see that they *are* tandems, in that the cause precedes the effect, and may therefore confidently be given the causal role in the linkage. The effect never precedes the cause. One occasionally comes across couplings in which the cause produces the effect so fast that they seem to act together, like pressing a light-switch and getting light in the room. Likewise, a fire in the hearth simultaneously warms the room. However, even when it is simultaneous, one knows that the fire is the cause, and the warming of the room is the effect. It would strain one's credulity and sense of temporal direction to assert the opposite, i.e., that the warming of the room is the cause of the fire.

In studying some of the North American Indian tribes, researchers like Boas, Sapir and Whorf suggested that a given language might not be only the *product* of certain ways of thinking, or of a particular culture, it might also have a *causative* role in determining those ways of thinking, or the prime characteristics of that culture. In other words, people use language this way and not another way because they see the world this way and not another way, and they see the world this way and not another way because they use language this way and not another way.

For example, why does the Eskimo language have the same construction for past and present? Why does English have different constructions for the antecedent past, the simple past and the past stretching to, and sometimes beyond, the present? Why doesn't English have a 'proper' construction for the future? Why does French use just one form for the simple and continuous? Why do some Red Indian speakers use different words for 'running water' and 'standing water', while English speakers need to join words together to get something like the same ideas? Are these ideas truly the same when they are expressed in such different ways?

It is possible that the past is not very important for Eskimo people, but that it is important enough for English speaking people for them to create different linguistic categories representing their perception of it. It is possible that French speaking people see no pressing need to differentiate between 'I think' and 'I am thinking', whereas English speakers find it useful to mark the difference.

But is this the real reason? The stronger likelihood is that English speakers or French speakers do or do not mark the difference simply because that is the way their respective languages work. English-speakers mark the difference primarily because the English language happens to mark the difference, and this makes it seem 'natural' to them. An English speaker fluent in French might move painlessly from marking the difference when he speaks in English, to leaving it unmarked when he speaks in French. There is nothing natural about either convention.

Further to this, it is possible that the past is relatively unimportant for some people because their language does not seem to give it a great deal of importance. A person's idea of the 'reality' of the world would tend to be coloured by the language he uses. Cause and effect become blurred in this self-sustaining cycle. One's naive understanding of the matter is that a language evolves in a certain way because the people who use it see the world in that way, and that they see the world in that way because of environmental or circumstantial happenings, the assumptions and beliefs that grow and harden in the struggle for survival, and the need to develop workable social systems. That is the logical progression. However, the repository of that society's culture and its strivings and beliefs is its language, and this has a formative and perpetuating influence on the society it evolves from.

Most people think that the language they use is an obvious, accurate and natural rendering of 'reality', and are puzzled or annoyed when they encounter other approaches to it. But, of course, there is no way of determining what *real* reality is. Nothing is truly objective; the individual looks out at the world through the screen of his own senses and interprets things according to his own language moulds. All facts are psychological, and are perceived through the linguistically shaped prisms of the brain. An example of linguistic relativism is how the 'third day from now' in some eastern languages means the third day including today, whereas in English the counting starts from tomorrow. Other examples might be culled from differing approaches in the use of prepositions. So also, the incomprehensible phenomenon of time, which might be subjected to a lot of ordering and dividing in one language, but treated in an off-hand, casual way in another. This could produce some human groups for whom time-consciousness and punctuality are primary concerns, and others for whom these things mean very little.

Whorf states the proposition as follows:

> We cut nature up, organize it into concepts, and ascribe significances as we do, largely because we are parties to an agreement to organize it in this way—an agreement that holds through our speech community and is codified in the patterns of our language.. .(4)

In one example, Whorf showed that what might be called a 'dripping spring' by English speakers is conceived by Apache speakers as 'water, or springs, whiteness moves downward', highlighting a considerable difference in concept and expression (5).

Writers like Clark and Clark seem uncomfortable with the proposition:

> ... unhappily, the evidence for the Sapir-Whorf hypothesis has been equivocal. Whorf's own work suffers all too often from the weakness evident in the last example. From his anecdotes, it is impossible to tell whether Indian and European languages cut up the world differently or not. Direct tests of the hypothesis have fared no better... (6)

However, writers like Mathiot support the proposition, though with pleas for more research into some of the basic questions raised by Boas (especially), Sapir and Whorf:

> ...language is conceived as a system with two separate dimensions, the grammatical and the lexical, each dimension being viewed as having a separate structure, i.e. as having units and relations, in its own right. Thus there are, on the one hand, grammatical units and grammatical relations, on the other hand, lexical units and lexical relations. Both dimensions manifest the referential function, i.e., they serve to refer to the phenomena differentiated by the culture in which the language is spoken. The difference between the two dimensions lies in the way in which this reference is made: In the

> grammatical dimension it is obligatory and to a large extent subconscious. In the lexical dimension it is optional and to a large extent deliberate... without a better substantive knowledge than we presently have of the meanings communicated through language, any further inquiry into the relation of language to world view, or into the relation of language to the rest of culture, runs the danger of being vacuous... (7)

Words, the lexis of a language, have an obvious though arbitrary referential function. What is understood from the foregoing is that grammatical formations have a similar function, at a more fundamental and compulsory level. Is it a particular 'world-view' that prompts some people to lump past and present constructions together in the language they speak? Why do other speakers have elaborate grammatical formations for the past and weak ones for the future? Why does one group of people put the verb in the middle of a sentence while another group puts it in the beginning, and another at the end, and yet another embed it in some other part of speech? Do they have different world-views? If indeed they do, this becomes a strong argument in favour of learning as many languages as possible in order to provide the brain with a multiplicity of world-views.

That language can affect thoughts and attitudes should not occasion scepticism or surprise. There are some defensible 'truths' in the way a language perceives the world. For example, if one says, 'this (thing) is a chair', one asserts not only the *chairness,* or the lexical naming of the thing, but its existence as well, from the grammatical construction used (though the copula 'be' is seldom used as an assertion of existence). In essence, this sentence states that 'there *is* something here, and all of us agree to call it a chair.' The assertion contains naming elements in the referential convention of the word 'chair', the primary lexical item in this sentence. It also contains a more fundamental reference in the grammatical assertion. One can derive confirmation for the rightness or wrongness of the assertion from other senses, such as touch, sight, etc., or from the agreement or disagreement expressed by others, assuming they belong to the same speech convention. The truth of linguistic assertions like this one can be confirmed or denied from independent and relatively concrete impressions.

However, there are a number of assertions that can be neither confirmed nor denied in a concrete way. Goblins, pixies, leprechauns, etc., exist, if they do at all, as linguistic 'truths'. When one says, 'this (thing) is a pixie ', one asserts the existence of something the existence of which cannot be demonstrated independently. Nevertheless, such linguistic truths have had, and continue to have, a lot of influence on human thinking in most societies. Medieval writing, some of which carried a lot of religious weight at that time, seems to show no hesitation or doubt about the reality and existence of *incubi* and *succubi,* unsupportable linguistic suppositions which would be given no credence today.

The point here is that demonstrable linguistic truths and undemonstrable linguistic truths have much the same effect on the 'world view' of a set of speakers. Both are clothed in language, and are presented to the brain as equally valid expositions of fact. Unless it is alert about these things, the brain is likely to accept both of them as such. Language not only refers to demonstrable things and happenings in the surrounding world, it also creates categories, tones, attitudes, facts and perspectives for that world.

The grammatical structures of a language etch the brain along certain route perceptions. The channels are different for speakers of different languages, though there are certainly some, and perhaps many, elements that overlap. In any case, the etchings can be either simple and elementary, or mature and complex. The theoretical basis of directed writing as a means of improving the brain's etchings, rests on assumptions like this one. With this power to mould the way the brain thinks about itself and the world at large, not only in naming things, but in its primary linguistic categories and structures as well, language would seem to have a strong formative factorability in brain development. It cannot increase native intelligence, which is huge anyway, but it might be able to set up mature patterns of thinking in the brain.

Writing has an advantage over speaking. The relative cognitive ability of literate and non-literate people was researched by a number of anthropologists between the nineteen fifties and nineteen seventies (8). Some of them maintained that the acquisition of literacy skills, the convention of text, meant relinquishing the assumptions of speaking—*text* is planned, *utterance* is spontaneous, indicating a qualitative difference between the two conventions. Sometimes, especially among adults trying to become literate, the transition between the convention of utterance to the convention of text is incomplete or imperfect. It was also postulated that literate people were better at reasoning than non-literate people. Although some of these studies were flawed, this hypothesis has continued to affect approaches to the teaching of writing:

> ...There is no evidence at all, that links style to cognitive ability. We simply have no valid reasons for believing that style has any effect whatsoever on either the way the mind operates or on the content of an essay. Nevertheless, this assumed connection has had a major impact on writing research and writing instruction... (9)

Writing and Mental Development

Amid the clamour of modern scientific jargon, Bacon's quiet observations tend to pass unnoticed. Speaking, he said, makes a ready man, reading a full man and writing an exact man, moving from language to man in a Whorfian sense, rather than from man to language. Practicing certain skills leads to certain mental abilities and attitudes.

Also unnoticed is the incompatibility between being 'ready' and being 'exact'. A rapid speaking ability gifted by good speech organs and a lot of practice, enables the brain to function rapidly in spoken language, if a bit fuzzily and within a relatively narrow lexical band. But, no matter how hard a man tries to increase his speed, the language producing process is much slower in writing. Using shorthand is good for note-taking; a person using it can keep up with normal speech most of the time. However, in the ordinary writing convention there is too much to think about in punctuation, spelling, lexis, structure and presentation. The mere fact of its slowness gives scope for greater accuracy and the use of a wider vocabulary.

It cannot be common, but there might be a few people who are linguistically both ready and exact, able to combine at one and the same time a fast but somewhat limited and not always accurate language producing mechanism, with a slow, wide, carefully organised one. The attitudes engendered by each mode are different. In tennis, the good base-liner is not usually a good net-volleyer. In language, the good speaker is not usually a good writer. Moving from one convention to another with equal facility is unlikely unless the individual has practised both conventions equally, and has a dual mind-set which inclines him to both simultaneously.

This is not impossible. It is not the researcher's intention to suggest that speaking and writing are incompatible, but it seems clear that they are not complementary. History has many examples of slow, hesitant, inefficient speakers who were very good at writing. Not much is known about Shakespeare, but he is the prime example of self-effacement, of what Keats called "the negative capability', in his writings. 'Poor speaking-good writing' is probably true of Dryden. And in comparatively recent times, T. S. Eliot serves as an example of a slow assembling of thoughts in speaking, as though he were imposing his 'writing' language producing mechanism on his 'speaking' language producing mechanism.

This has been discussed to strengthen the argument that developing certain language skills can produce certain mental and attitudinal channels in the brain. Writing's ability to 'make' an 'exact' man in the Baconian sense is discussed in this section. Some of writing's special virtues in the process have already been pointed out. It is deliberative; of the four skills it has the slowest tempo, so it is well suited for controlling and grooving the brain's natural tendency to jump about; it gives the writer opportunities to think about things, and select what he considers to be the best expression for them; it can be changed or corrected a dozen times if the writer so desires; it puts things down as a permanent record, imposing less strains on the parallel short term memory than speaking or listening; overall control of expression is superior in writing, because the writer can see how he started and how he ought to finish, something all too often lost in the ephemera of speaking.

Some theoretical positions were established or at least proposed and given general support in the nineteen sixties. Writing rather than speech was seen as the more accurate manifestation of cognitive maturity (10). The Baconian or Whorfian inversion, that teaching students how to manipulate longer clauses and sentences could hasten linguistic maturity, became the basis of writing instruction in many institutions in America, a practice that continues till today. It is claimed that the technique described as 'sentence combining' has proved its worth in improving a writer's control over his medium. Since there is a mechanical element, a beginner whose understanding of the language is still unsure, gains confidence from the technique itself, once he sees how it is done. A typical elementary exercise might have two statements:

a.   The light is hanging from the roof

b.   The light has a green shade

Leading to, 'the light which has a green shade is hanging from the roof' or 'the light which is hanging from the roof has a green shade', since both combinations are possible and logical. This helps to show that language is flexible, and that a succession of ideas can be expressed in concise, though complex, constructions.

More advanced exercises would require deletion to minimum possibilities of expression. The first combined sentence would require a change of the 'which' clause to an adjectival 'with a green shade', becoming 'the light with a green shade is hanging from the roof', and the second could remove the 'which' construction while retaining its implication, 'the light hanging from the roof has a green shade'. The use of transformational functions can result in expression which is both correct and succint.

A more advanced exercise might have several items:

a.   De Forest perfected the first effective vacuum tube

b.   De Forest was an American inventor

c.   The vacuum tube was an important development for radio technology

The end product might look like 'De Forest, an American inventor, perfected an important development for radio technology, the first effective vacuum tube', or ' De Forest, an American inventor, perfected the first effective vacuum tube, an important development for radio technology.'

More subtle exercises can be introduced:

a. I was judging the heavy clouds

b. I thought it would rain in half an hour

This could be neatly combined and reduced to

Judging from the heavy clouds, I thought it would rain in half an hour

A certain ability to see how clauses relate to each other, and to pare away the excess construction required by whole sentences so that ideas can be put inside or embedded in the base structure is required, and is soon learnt with a little practice.

Combinations of a causal or temporal nature can also be attempted, in which students discern how one statement leads causally to another, or in which one statement follows another.

a. John worked sixteen hours a day

b. John became a rich man

This has an element of causality, and would lead to a combination like:

Because John worked sixteen hours a day, he became rich

(or)

John became rich because he worked sixteen hours a day

And again:

c.   He went to Lahore

d.   He went to Sialkot

Not much causality is visible here, so a student would introduce a sequence, like:

> **First he went to Lahore, then he went to Sialkot**
>
> (or)
>
> **He went to Lahore before he went to Sialkot**
>
> (or)
>
> **He went to Sialkot after he went to Lahore**

Modifying details could be added to form cumulative sentences:

> **Asad went to Lahore, driving slowly and keeping his eyes on the road, singing to himself to stay awake, moving his body every now and then to exercise his muscles, etc.**

William comments on this approach as follows:

> It was noted that many students find an element of fun in figuring out different ways to join sentences together. The task has a puzzle-like fascination. Even more important, teachers began to see that sentence combining seemed to improve writing performance. Students

who practiced it gained greater control over their sentences and were able to develop more variety in sentence types...These classroom observations have been supported by many studies showing that students who engage in regular sentence-combining exercises increase the length of their T-units and improve overall composition quality...(11)

Sentence combining could certainly be used in conjunction with more formal sentence exercises. These might have as their objectives the changing of base forms to negatives or interrogatives, the strengthening of agreement of subject and verb, shifting elements, time elements, complementation, expansion, or, in fact, any part of sentence construction that might seem to need strengthening in any given class of students. A lot will depend on the judgement of the teacher on the spot.

To be expected was a movement to discredit this approach and a series of studies to show that the gains produced by sentence-combining were short-lived. Here it should be stated that sentence combining is not some great new discovery. Exercises in combining have always been used in schools, long before the movement started, though perhaps not very systematically. The objection is that they focus too much on language at the sentence rather than the discourse level:

...along these lines, Kinneavy (1979) and Witte(1980) argue that the gains in T-unit length and writing quality attributed to sentence combining may actually be the result of teaching rhetorical principles like analysis and synthesis inductively, principles that are inherent in the process of combining. If this is the case, teaching these principles directly, no doubt through the associated rhetorical modes, would probably be more efficient. In other words, it may well be that teachers can have a significant effect on syntactic maturity and writing performance simply by focusing more attention on more demanding tasks, such as analysis and argument...(12)

There is an element of circularity about this argument, namely, that linguistic maturity can be stimulated or accelerated by focusing on linguistically mature teaching activities. Also, the researcher is not sure that analysis and synthesis can be *taught,* as these processes are inherent in the brain's primary, pre-linguistic categories. Without some of these primary categories the brain would not be able to begin the assault on knowledge. The brain is analysing and synthesising things all the time, whether it is taught to do so or not. Very little would be acquired or understood by the individual, if he did not already possess as part of his native mental endowment the ability to analyse and synthesise things. There would be no distillation and formation of concepts out of percepts, no reductions, no expansions, no classification. However, students can certainly be made aware of them. Some of these issues will be discussed in the next chapter.

The implications of the foregoing are (a) that illiterate people have two of the language skills, but are handicapped because they do not have the other two language tools at their disposal, and (b) that this is a big handicap: the skill of speaking confines them to the immediate, the performative and the concrete, and (c) that they are less able to function effectively in analytical and abstract modes of thinking than literate people.

The implications for Pakistan are profound. This country's culture is still oral. A reasonable estimate of literacy at this point in history is forty to forty-five per cent, of which about half might be dismissed as being so rudimentary that no writing is likely to emerge from it. Only half of the residual half is likely to go on to higher levels. The dominant mind-set in the country is attuned almost entirely to the skills, thinking modes and attitudes of listening and speaking, and of speaking much more than listening. It dominates even those who have become literate, many of whom, despite their acquired skills, will never really make a full transition to the literacy mode of thinking, simply because the climate around them is so overwhelmingly oral.

Thinking in Pakistan is basically confined to the kind of mentation associated with oracy skills. Literacy, the habits of literacy, the attitudes of literacy and above all, *the possibilities in ordered and abstract thinking* opened up by literacy, are denied to most of the population. The advantages of literacy are inestimable. With the present unbalanced ratio in the country, the small percentage of people who are literate cannot make much impact. Societal and attitudinal changes are likely to become visible when the ratio values change in favour of literacy. To hasten this, an immediate, strong and sustained effort should be made for high literacy rates.

Chapter 7 Notes

1. Williams, 122-123

2. Ibid., 123

3. Bryson, 11-13

4. Clark and Clark, 557

5. Ibid.,

6. Ibid., 554-555

7. Mathiot, M., *Ethnolinguistics: Boas, Sapir and Whorf Revisited,* Mouton Publishers, the Hague, 1979, ix

8. This is based on a discussion in Williams, 121-123

9. Ibid., 123

10. Hunt, K., "Grammatical Structures Written at Three Grade Levels", *National Council of Teachers of English, No* 3, 1965. Hunt established a relationship between rising levels of maturity and the ability to write longer and more mature sentences.

11. Williams, 127

12. Ibid., 129

Chapter Eight

The Classroom and the Teacher

It is said that a few weeks in a foreign country where the language one wants to learn is used for everyday communication and commerce is better than several months or even years spent in a classroom. This might be true for listening and speaking skills, because the learner finds himself involved in natural, real life situations, asking the way, buying things, arguing over prices, and so on. An alert person would soon open a few windows for interaction. However, the skills of reading and writing require some direction, since they are less natural and are best learnt in a classroom.

In chapter six it was suggested that sentence combining techniques could prove useful for improving the stylistic maturity of people who can write and who have some English at their command. At the same time it was stated that success in sentence combining might not be the *causal* factor in the process, but a *concomitant* of yet more fundamental mental activities such as analysing and synthesising, a 'matter generates form' approach.

Williams describes these as rhetorical principles (l). Further, he suggests that the 'top-down' approach to writing likely to be stimulated by sentence combining and the focus on surface elements of style might be found wanting in the final analysis (2). Elements of the 'bottom-up' approach related to content, meaning and purpose, tend to be ignored or taken for granted, things that will fall in place by themselves.

Nevertheless, the top-down approach continues to be popular because it gives both student and teacher something immediate, visible and tangible to work with. Proponents of this approach claim that sentence combining exercises open up modes of discovery that help students in the pursuit of ideas, a 'form generates matter' approach. However, writers like Williams state that there is as yet no irrefutable evidence for this claim (3).

How much can style influence content, and how much does content imply or generate style? How much do clothes 'make' the man, and how much do clothes depend on the man? One's naive instinct moves from content to style, the bottom-up approach, that a person first has some ideas and then proceeds to clothe those ideas in language. Substance surely takes, or ought to take, precedence in this pairing of matter and form. However, reverting to earlier arguments, purpose, content and meaning, even thinking itself, are inextricably bound to the kind of language used to express these elements, so to that extent at least, style *is* content.

One sees the language. One never actually sees the content. It is not possible to guess those 'bottom' elements, except through an interpretation of the language used for them. The arguments seem good on both sides. There is little likelihood of certitudes in such arguments: one is forced into a kind of relativism. However, some of these issues lead to a point of theoretical paralysis that is not helpful for a teacher in his effort to supply students with handholds in the slippery climb to second language adequacy.

It is suggested that both approaches be kept as a background framework in planning classroom activities. Four points may be kept in mind here: (a) that mechanical applications such as simple sentence combining exercises, with a minimum of mental involvement, are useful in the beginning because they increase confidence, (b) that a successful mastery of such, and later of more advanced applications, probably stimulates exploratory categories and directions in the brain, though there is no clear evidence for this, (c) that the more the brain works at later stages, the better it is likely to be for the writing process, and (d) that, since no language is involved, there is no way of determining what the brain does in a pre-language mould, though it may be safely assumed that a lot of pre-language activity does take place and that this activity is crucial to the brain's language producing ability.

The First Phase

The primary understanding of the situation should be that, while the teacher's job is to move his students slowly away from an essentially Urdu ethos, towards an essentially English one, a total transference is unlikely. It is also unnecessary. There are some advantages to be discovered in maintaining the bilingual base. There is nothing wrong with the Urdu mind-frame, nor is its imposition on the English mind-frame likely to damage the latter. Native English speakers have their own way of doing things. Native Urdu speakers have a different way of doing the same things in English, and there is nothing better or worse in the difference.

Here, the emphasis is on 'mind-frame' rather than 'language-frame'. One does not have to think like an Anglo-Saxon in order to use his language unless one wants to use it exactly as he does. That an Urdu speaker, or a bilingual speaker, should seek to use English exactly like a monolingual Englishman seems to be a denial of a basic advantage; it seems like an unnecessary self-limitation. English can be enriched with inputs from other users of the language. Conrad's writing in English might not always be quite 'English' in the way it is used, but it is admirably flexible and expressive. Legouis and Cazamian have written an introduction to English literature in a kind of English prose some people might describe as fulsome or syrupy; but it is entirely readable and very informative.

In the early nineteen seventies, Kaplan introduced some ideas about pathways of thinking characterised in different groups of people (4). There is a rhetorical linearity in Anglo-Saxon thinking which sets it against the circularity, parallelism, tangentialism or helicity one might discover in some other cultures:

> Kaplan's analysis carries no value judgement; each rhetorical pattern is valid within its particular culture. Thus we cannot object to the digressions of the Spanish pattern, for

example; to do so would be the equivalent to objecting to the Mexican fondness for spicy foods. We can only note that the pattern is different from what we find in English... (5)

Since the need to write is prompted by a need to communicate, it is probably unwise to insist too much on Anglo-Saxon patterns in the early stages. It might also be unwise to insist on those patterns at later stages. A Pakistani student can give interesting perspectives of his own. If he can do it in ways he is used to without incurring penalties for being 'un-English', the chances are that his communicative impulses will not be unduly inhibited.

No Kaplan has arisen in Pakistan to discuss the rhetorical patterns of Urdu. The difficulties are compounded because, while all Pakistanis speak Urdu when they need to, or want to, Urdu is not the primary language of communication for most Pakistanis (somewhere between eighty and ninety per cent), who use other Pakistani languages most of the time at home or work. Nevertheless as the dominant language in the region, its influence on Pakistani patterns is significant.

The following observations are offered. They are based on the author's personal experience rather than on scientific evaluation. A proper analysis of several texts in Urdu, and of English writings by Pakistani authors, is desirable to confirm or deny their validity. That will not be attempted in this short work.

(a) The paragraph formation of Urdu is different from that of English. A paragraph in Urdu occurs when the writer feels like a change, or if he feels that his block of writing has become too large for comfort. The concept is not inherent in the eastern tradition of writing, and might even have resulted from English influences in the region. Sometimes there are no paragraphs at all, even over extended pieces of writing. Only rarely will an Urdu paragraph display the typical 'topic-sentence-plus-supporting-statements' characteristics of the English paragraph.

(b) Punctuation is a concept grafted on Urdu, possibly because of the influence of English in the region. The basic indication of a pause in Urdu is a quick dash, which is used for a comma or a full stop as desired. Urdu has no capital letters, no markers of proper nouns, no colons or semi-colons, no apostrophes, and, until it took its cues from European languages, no inverted commas, question marks or exclamation marks. The absorption of English conventions in punctuation does not come easily or naturally. Special problems are found with capitalisation. An Urdu speaker might omit them where they ought to be used, or, in some kind of compensatory zeal, insert them where they are not required at all, when he writes in English.

(c) The idea of a beginning, a middle and an end is not interpreted in quite the same way in Urdu. Despite the teacher's frequent appeals for strict relevance, many Pakistani students feel uncomfortable when are pushed into a direct confrontation with a topic. Long, indirect and sometimes barely relevant preambles are preferred, as being culturally more acceptable. The English way seems rather blunt and socially clumsy to them.

(d) Urdu thinking is not as linear as that of English. If one were to use something like Kaplan's observations, ideas in Urdu tend to run in parallel, or are stacked up and then released in blocks, or are drawn back and forth over the text. The presentation is often quite subtle, but it rarely runs in a sequenced line, as in English.

(e) Urdu writing is not excessively digressive, but it tends to be more so than English.

(f) Being primarily a literary language, Urdu tends towards a 'high' selection of words in written form. Sometimes very ordinary, mundane needs are expressed in a heavily Persianised or Arabised vocabulary, as though there is a determination to make it incomprehensible for ordinary people. This tendency is carried over to English writing. There is a fundamental difference here. Urdu is not used very much as a vehicle for science and technology. English is an 'information' language in many of its functions, though it has an equally well developed literary side. English writing has been moulded since the eighteenth century by a practical need to report and explain things in science and technology. By trial and error, it has developed certain ways for accommodating this need, and these ways have crossed over to business, commerce and government writing, as well. One need only compare mid-nineteenth century with mid-twentieth century government and business documents, to see the difference. It is much less given to ornamentation, and more likely to follow conventions in planning, lexis and formatting designed to aid rather than hinder the quick transference of knowledge.

(g) If general characteristics are to be hazarded, the Urdu sensibility tends to be lyrical, recyclic, instinctive, loosely structured and ornamental: while the English sensibility, when it is not being used for emotionally expressive purposes, is matter-of-fact, planned, structured, bare and sequenced.

(h) Although Urdu writing represents the literate segment of this nation, it is still affected by the oral expectations of the much larger illiterate segment of the population. On the other hand, English writing today caters to reading populations of nations that are widely literate, wherever you find them. As mentioned earlier, the expectations are different in literate and illiterate, or literate and semi-literate, societies.

If these observations are true or even partly true there is a considerable difference in the understanding of the writing art in the two language conventions.

An English reader might find a piece of writing by a student formless and badly sequenced. However, if one overlooks the surface mistakes and strangeness of approach, some kind of pattern emerges. But it is not an English pattern. It is an attempt at communication with regard to some aspects of Milton's seventeenth century

Paradise Lost seen through the eyes of a young, twenty-first century Urdu speaker, diffidently trying to express himself in written English. The ideas and language are his own, qualities so rare in this kind of writing that the piece stands out. The researcher did not ask for it, which puts it into the *intrinsically* motivated category. It was proffered spontaneously by the student.

The teacher has some options here: (a) he can make a contemptuous rejection of the whole thing as garbled, repetitive and shot with language errors; (b) he can focus entirely on the correction of surface and planning errors, to the exclusion of content, ignoring the all-important communicational impulse behind the writing; or, (c) he can overlook some of the apparent formlessness as the product of local patterns of expression, read through the whole thing to look for developments, restatements and conclusions, and point out the surface mistakes in a non-punitive way. This was what the researcher tried to do, circling them without comment, in order to draw the student's attention to them. The hope was that on reflection, he would see some of the anomalies for himself, and if not, that he would ask others, or the researcher himself, to explain them. This option was adopted in order to preserve this student's desire to communicate in writing.

One result was a fair output of writing by this student in particular. He continued to make mistakes in spelling and grammar, but in diminishing quantities. His self-confidence increased. Since the researcher's primary aim was to get a lot of writing done, the option seemed to have merit.

Sample A should be compared with sample B by the same student, offered ten days later.

The researcher has used this approach with fair success with other students as well— *quantity* rather than quality, at least in the beginning; correction as *self-correction,* as far as possible; *refinements* to come later. The time-bracket for these activities straddles one semester at least, and may require two, or even more. Some students who come into the programme as poor writers, never progress to really good writing, but most become better as they go along.

> Although many more investigations are needed in this area, Kaplan's work has received support from several research studies. Jones (1982) and Jones and Tetroe (1983), for example, examined the writing of bilingual students in Canada and established that syntactic, rhetorical, and planning skills in students' first language transferred, with little change, to their second language. Harder (1984), also studying bilingual students in Canada, obtained similar findings. He concluded that complex communicational difficulties... "cannot be explained as merely insufficient knowledge of English grammar, diction or idiom. Such problems do not involve linguistic differences in the native (NL) and target language (TL) but encompass different stylistic habits, different ways of thinking, and different cultural values"(p.l 15) (6)

While there is no need to remove altogether the Urdu

flavour of Pakistani writing in English, many students are anxious to get something close to English writing. What might be seen as interesting variations by one kind of reader, will be seen as un-English errors by another kind, and this they are anxious to avoid. There is no harm in progressing in this direction. The native world view can still peep through local writing in good English, much as Conrad's 'Polish soul', if it is possible to talk about such a thing, shows through some of his writing:

> ... With age he had put on flesh a little, had increased his girth like an old tree presenting no symptoms of decay; and even the opulent, lustrous ripple of white hairs upon his chest seemed an attribute of unquenchable vitality and vigour...

> ... He nourished the hope that this five hundred would perhaps be the means, if everything else failed, of obtaining some work which, keeping his body and soul together (not a matter of great outlay), would enable him to be of use to his daughter.. .(7)

Slightly old-fashioned for the early part of the twentieth century? Slightly convoluted and ornamental? So what? It is entirely readable.

Does a 'French' soul inform the following? Quiller-couch (8) seems to think a 'Gallic', and therefore un-English, instinct impels Cazamian towards looking for neat categories for what is essentially whimsical in English literature:

.. .Engrossed in its own affairs or propagating its ideas throughout Europe, revolutionary and imperial France is almost entirely absorbed in active interests, leaving to its political exiles, to a Madame de Stael or a de Villiers, the opportunity of gathering the germs of foreign influence which the Romantic England, on the contrary, on the contrary, shaken as it is by the storm of events in France.. .(9)

Another example is given here, taken from the English writings of an author of mixed Ceylonese/Dutch parentage living in Canada:

...Palipana could move within archeological sites as if they were his own historical homes from past lives—he was able to guess the existence of a water gardens location, unearth it, fill it with white lotus. He worked for years on the royal parks around Aburadhapura and Kandy.. ..(10)J

Yet another example comes from a Pakistani writer:

...Silence is creative, and recreative. It is restful and calming. In relating to and understanding its sublime subtleties, one needs to bear in mind the critical difference and distinction between solitude and loneliness. The former is 'Takhliya', and the latter, 'Tanhai' in Urdu, Pakistan's national language. The former is spiritual; the latter, secular.. .(11)

If anything un-English shows through the foregoing examples, it does not matter at all. The control of the English language is complete.

One example of early twentieth century native English writing is introduced to set against the previous ones:

> ...I stopped in front of the Villa Rossa. The shutters were up but it was still going on inside. Somebody was singing. I went on home. Rinaldi came in while I was undressing...(12)

This is Hemingway. His 'muscular', 'deceptively simple' style of writing, has received a lot of critical approval. Whatever its merits, it typifies the twentieth century trend in native English writing; short, direct sentences, simple, active, affirmative statements, frequent full-stops but very few commas (none in this group of sentences), hardly any modifiers (none in this group of sentences), hardly any connectors, hardly any 'presence' of the author in what he writes, all put into a sequential pattern which causes no strain, because it is chronologically or logically plausible.

This kind of writing is said to clarify meaning by going to the bald expression, almost down to the kernel sentences, of the author's basic ideation and purpose. Excesses, frills, digressions, attempts to impress the reader, long, convoluted sentences and strange words are eschewed.

Modern computers are programmed to help writers on much the same assumptions. Users will notice that sentences longer than about fifteen words, and the passive voice, immediately bring on the computer's warnings. It is said that the reader's brain takes a little longer to decode and comprehend the passive voice in comparison with the active voice. The simple, active, affirmative declaration, stated in eight to ten words with minimal punctuational digression and interference, is the most readily comprehended and the least likely to be misinterpreted.

Yet people who write within the stylistic constraints of the computer are likely to produce flat pieces. This researcher, at least, is not at all enthused by Hemingway's kind of studied, planned, whittled down writing. Punctuation can certainly be pared down with advantage to the reader. Nineteenth century writing suffered because of an excess of commas and capital letters. But sentence length should grow organically from the underlying thought process; it cannot be fixed arbitrarily without damaging that process. Also, the passive voice, apart from its extensive use in scientific writing, is much too useful in far too many situations to be abandoned as though it were an error.

If a Pakistani prefers to write 'your goodself or 'your goodselves' instead of 'you' it is because English has only one option in the second person for degrees of formality, while Urdu has three. It is because the Urdu approach to things tends to be oblique rather than direct, and because it demands markers of respect.

This is not a fault. It is an instinctively different way of doing things engendered by linguistic and cultural differences. This author can see no good reason for denying one's own cultural underpinnings simply because one is attempting to write in another language. English has one advantage over all other languages today. As a world language, it is no longer the strict and exclusive preserve of any group of speakers. True, one still comes across native English speakers, anxious to maintain the old positions of legislative eminence, who loftily dismiss anything that sounds strange to them. However, the language has really outgrown such people.

The teacher's primary role in the beginning is motivational, to encourage the growth of the flower, to tend it carefully once it has come forth, and to position it so that other flowers can grow out of it. All student writing should be supported. It matters little in the beginning if the rhetorical patterns of Urdu or other Pakistani languages are used for the process, though in line with the researcher's initial proposition that Pakistani English writing should become more like that of international English writing, the student should not be allowed to remain in those patterns forever.

The Second Phase

Once a degree of confidence and a readiness to communicate are established, some movement forward to a more 'English' way of writing English may be undertaken. Senior students cannot get away with spelling, punctuation and grammar inconsistencies for too long. Writing is rightly conceived as a mental process, and transferring to an English mode can be boosted initially from writing habits already acquired in the native language: somewhat like using a good battery to jump-start a car whose battery is wired into the system, but is not yet charged enough to function by itself.

There are some mechanical, or only marginally mental, aspects of English writing that must be practised and mastered. The teacher can start with pointing, or punctuation. Here, also, the process should not be inhibited by excessive rule-giving. Punctuation has a lot to do with the writer's instinctive feeling for pauses, sentence-length and the beginnings or endings of paragraphs, and the Urdu writer's instinct for these things will be different. Subjecting this feeling to rigidly restrictive categories can lead to the rather dead and artificial style of writing seen earlier. The Pakistani context is primary in these considerations. Nevertheless, the full stop, the comma, the capital letter and the question mark are basic to the understanding of English writing.

The Full Stop

The full stop is not the equivalent of the dash in Urdu. Its basic purpose is to show the completion of a sentence that is not interrogative or exclamatory in nature. For such sentences the question mark and exclamation mark is used.

At one time it was placed *inside* and not *outside* a quotation mark or inverted comma at the end of a sentence, but this cannot possibly matter. It should not be made into yet another meaningless, anxiety generating convention.

At one time it was obligatory to use it for the abbreviations Mr., Mrs., Rev., Dr., or M.D., but this is optional now. Abbreviations such as U.S.A., U.K., A.M. and P.M. are seen sometimes with and sometimes without the full stop, but B.C. and AD. always have it, at least in this researcher's experience. It serves no sensible purpose in any of the examples given here. Omitting it would make for cleaner writing.

Other than for its primary purpose, the modern

trend is to use the full stop for as few ancillary functions as possible. Too much by way of dots, points and markers can be scattered across a page of writing. This general trend is good for those whose developed writing ability is in the loose pointing system of a language like Urdu. Pointing has its obvious uses, but at one time, especially in the eighteenth and nineteenth centuries, it became an elaborate scholastic mythology, an additional neurosis for the second language student already perplexed by the difficult process of writing in English.

The Comma

Of even greater importance than the full stop, the comma can be misused to a degree that seriously affects both meaning and the flow of language. The following is a sample of the older concept of comma usage in writing:

> ...Nothing has contributed so much, and so universally, to the corruption of delivery, as the bad use, which has been made, of the modern art of punctuation, by introducing artificial tones into all sentences, to the exclusion of the natural; for the teacher of the art of reading, in order to distinguish, with greater accuracy, the stops from each other in utterance, annexed to them different notes to the voice, as well as different portions of time.. .(13)

The following is from the nineteenth century:

> ... It is, indeed, a strange art to take these blocks, rudely conceived for the market or the

> bar, and by tact and application, touch them
> to the finest meanings and distinctions, restore
> them to their primal energy, wittily shift them
> to another issue, or make them a drum to rouse
> the passions...(14)

Commas have not disappeared from English writing. About half as many are used today as were used in earlier times. Sheridan's mistake in (14) was in thinking of reading as recitation. As a dramatist his first concern would have been the spoken word, no doubt. However, more and more it has been realised that writing should not limit itself by trying to be a mere visual rendering of the spoken word. Those who try to imitate too closely the speaking voice in their writing can inhibit or distort the potential of the medium. Trying to copy spoken tones, regional dialects, pronunciational quirks or conversational idiosyncrasies often fails in writing:

> "...Grayson, stay behind—umph—after the rest."

Then:

> "Grayson, I don't want to be—umph—severe, because you are generally pretty good—umph—in your work, but to-day—you don't seem—umph—to have been trying at all.'(15)

This is clumsy and not at all convincing. The writing medium has taken some time to realise that it is more effective when it understands what it can do with itself, than when it borrows characteristics from other media.

The marking functions of the comma may be summed up as follows:

(a) To introduce small pauses in a sentence (only if deemed necessary by the writer; it is probably better to write, 'it is indeed a strange art...' than, 'it is, indeed, a strange art...')

(b) To mark a series of modifiers linked to the same noun ('He is an energetic, talkative, quick-thinking young man')

(c) To mark segments of thought in combined ideas. They would be used in sentence combining exercises ('John Milton, the author of the most famous epic in English literature, Paradise Lost, died in 1674')

(d) To mark parentheses ('Exercise, when done in moderation, is beneficial for the health')

(e) To mark repetitions of words, or of words with the same meaning ('Shut, shut, the door good John...'/ 'Cease, desist, I say...')

(f) To mark a quotation shown in the same statement ('Whenever he comes he says, "Good day to all of you..."')

(g) To mark different words in a series ('Wealth, power, prominence, these were his main interests')

(h) To put pairs of words together ('Clever or stupid, important or unimportant, big or small, all people are equal before the law')

(i) To avoid repeating certain words ('speaking makes a ready man; reading, a full man; writing, an exact man')

(j) To mark inversions ('Of all boxers, Muhammad Ali is the best')

(k) To mark prenominal disjuncts of attitude, style and point of view ('Unfortunately, I can't see the point of this argument'/ 'In truth, I can't see the point of this argument'/ 'Politically, much has to be done to strengthen the nation's institutions')

(l) To mark intrusive connectors ('He did, however, meet his elder brother when he went to Lahore')

These are offered as a general guide. The teacher might have his own preferences, or he may ascribe to older recommendations in this regard. Older writing can still be read, but it sometimes looks jerky.

It is probably useful to show students how usage can affect meaning. A series could be built around a simple statement like:

He drank a cup of tea

This could then be marked with commas to emphasise various items in the sentence:

He, (not someone else) drank a cup of tea

He drank, (he did not make) a cup of tea

He drank a cup, (not a glass) of tea

and so on. Difficulties caused by marking can also be shown:

He is, frankly, a liar

This means that, in the candid opinion of the *writer,* the subject is a liar. However,

He is frankly a liar

could mean the same, or it could mean that the *subject* does not bother to hide his propensity for lying.

Also:

Doing things right is, by no means, more difficult than doing things wrong.

The effect of the commas here is to isolate and bracket the phrase 'by no means'. Yet there is an obvious continuity from one side of the statement to the other. No commas are indicated here. The sentence falls into place much better without them:

Doing things right is by no means more difficult than doing things wrong.

These demonstrations can be reinforced by a series of exercises. As with most things in language, habit and familiarity are the best determiners. Exercises like the following, which, depending on what aspect of punctuation is being taught, need not insist on capital letters, full stops or other punctuation marks, are well-known. Number 'c' is quite difficult, as all kinds of marks are required:

(a) some people say that sergeants are the most important people in the army this may or may not be true but certainly sergeant aslam the recruiting supervisor thought so

(b) he has written four essays evenings in karachi mornings in lahore my ambition in life and hobbies he will show them to the teacher tomorrow

(c) aslam accused jamshed of cheating during the exams when asked jamshed said what nonsense aslam cant talk like that about anyone because hes the one who cheats whenever he gets a chance he brought a sheet of paper into the hall yesterday and swallowed it when the invigilator passed I said you cant prove that now can you and he replied of course 1 cant hes destroyed the evidence but you are willing to tell the principal about this arent you I asked no he said

An exercise like 'c' can be used progressively, to accommodate more and more pointing marks as confidence increases. In the beginning it might be better not to pack too much into one or two exercises. Skill acquisition takes time.

Such exercises are useful for another purpose as well. If some languages can do without these marks and still make sense, why not English? One reason is that English has lost many of its inflections and might need more assistance in establishing a context than inflected languages like Urdu. However, a lot of it has to do with expectation and habit. A reading of such exercises usually reveals what the author means, regardless of the presence or absence of punctuation marks. If this were not so, it would not be possible to punctuate them. From this it is may be gathered that pointing is helpful, but not always essential. It is an aggravating area of writing for the foreign student.

The Capital Letter

The teacher will soon notice that some students, even senior ones, have only a hazy notion of capitalisation in English. The concept does not exist at all in Urdu. That the first word in a new sentence in English starts with a capital letter should be visible to all. That it is used for many other things might need reinforcement. That it should not be used whimsically would need to be iterated.

Capital letters are used:

(a) At the beginning of each new sentence.

(b) At the beginning of each new line of poetry (this is not always true of modern poetry).

(c) For proper nouns, i.e., John, Aslam, etc

(d) For adjectives derived from proper nouns, i.e., French literature.

(e) For the first person singular in the subject but not in the object case, 'That was the day I spoke to him,' but not, 'That was the day he spoke to Me'. Like most other things in language, this cannot be explained. It can only be asserted as a requirement established by convention. Some modern poets have deliberately reduced the first person singular to a small 'i' on the premise that it looks excessively egotistical when written with the capital I. What happens is that it becomes even more prominent because it flouts the convention. Logic has little to do with any of this.

(f) For divine names, such as God, the Absolute, the Beneficent.

(g) For the interjection '0, woe is me" and for the rare direct address, '0 Prince, O Chief...' (vocative)

(h) For large areas which are based on vague concepts of social conditions rather than actual physical location, i.e., the West, the South, the Third World. Some people do not use capital letters for such concepts. This author's preference is for small letters

(i) For letter abbreviations and acronyms, i.e. UNO, WHO, UNICEF, etc. These have proliferated over the last half century. Some of them are no longer acronyms but are now words in their own right.

This makes nine cases for the use of the capital letter alone. Added to what happens in full-stops and commas, conventions in punctuation rapidly build up into a large and complicated body of usage. Yet more is required. Another important mark, the question mark, must also be considered in the first phase for writing in English.

The Question Mark

Urdu has the same mark facing the other way. However, this does not make the transference any easier. Urdu forms questions in a different way from English. This is one area of considerable concern for the English language teacher in general and for the teacher of writing in particular. Within the limitations of this study it is assumed that the student knows how to ask questions in English. He might still have trouble showing those questions in writing, especially in indirect speech. A lot of practice is indicated.

Some conventions are suggested here:

(a) The question mark is used at the end of a question, and no other mark (such as a full stop) is required after it to indicate the end of the utterance, e.g., 'Did Aslam go to Lahore?'/ 'What did Aslarn do?' It is also used for questions formed by tag inversions, e.g., "Aslam went to Lahore, didn't he?'

(b) When a continuous utterance has many implied questions in a series, a single question mark may be placed at the end of the series, e.g., 'Is it mind, matter or something else?' However, some writers prefer to mark off each question separately, 'Is it mind? Matter? Or something else⁹' No recommendation is given here. As a general rule of thumb, the less the reader's eye has to contend with points on a written page, the better.

(c) It may be used to raise doubts about a statement by putting it in brackets, e.g., 'This candidate says he is an honest (?) worker for the great (?) cause.'

(d) It is used as follows if a statement leads to a question   continuously, "Have you thought about the man who says, 'I promise to remove poverty from this country'?"

The discussion has centred on only four kinds of marks so far. English has other marks. However, since they are not used so extensively the teacher might think it wise to introduce them later, to ease the clutter which otherwise ensues. Instruction in punctuation tends towards overloading the student with a shower of conventions and examples. The basic marks are the ones indicated above. If these are used well a lot of writing can be undertaken with confidence.

The other marks of English writing are summarised below:

1. *The semicolon* (;). This gives a longer pause and a more emphatic division than the comma. It may be used to mark complete ideas that are not entirely separated from other ideas, e.g., 'You may print five hundred copies of this book; five of them might be read; two might be purchased.'

2. *The colon* (:). This is more emphatic than the semicolon, but falls short of the full stop in applying closure to an idea. It is useful for balancing clauses or putting them in opposition to each other, e.g., 'Man proposes: God disposes'.

3. *The exclamation mark* (!). This is used for expressive purposes, e.g., 'How lovely the sky looks!' Nineteenth century writing tended towards a lot of robust expression, but it is better to use this mark sparingly

4. *The parenthesis* (( )). This is useful for isolating

an idea or for introducing a new idea into a statement without disturbing its general flow. 'It is said (but not by everyone) that active sentences are easier to comprehend than passive ones.'

5. *The dash* (—). The long dash can introduce a sudden reversal of thought, a special emphasis or a dramatic pause. Placed at both ends of an interpolation, it has a parenthetical function as well.

6. *The hyphen* (-). This is a short dash placed between words linked together to form single expressions. It appeared a lot in nineteenth and early twentieth century writing. It is probably redundant. If the words are linked they can be shown as one word. Or they may be shown as separate words. The reader will see 'full stop' written as 'fullstop' or 'full-stop' in different texts. The dash is a troublesome mark. Another function is to divide a word at the end of a line to run over to the next line. It is better to carry the whole word over to the next line. The researcher's recommendation is for the virtual elimination of this mark as it does very little for a text.

7. *The apostrophe* ('). This is needed for the Saxon possessive, e.g., 'This is Salim's car.' For some reason, as mentioned in chapter three, Pakistani students have begun to use it for the plural, e.g., 'All the Salim's in the room please stand up' instead of 'All the Salims in the room please stand up'. Deliberate remediation is required for this mark. Another function is to indicate the

omission of a letter in compressed forms like 'you're' (you are) or 'don't' (do not). Students regularly write 'your' for 'you're'.

8. *Inverted commas* ("). In the author's childhood the double inverted comma appeared outside the single one if there was a quotation within a quotation. The reverse is often seen nowadays. It should not matter either way if it is done consistently.

This author prefers the bare minimum when it comes to pointing. The eye is distressed by an excess of dots, dashes and capital letters suddenly appearing out of the blue in some texts. The trend for cleaner writing belongs to the twentieth century, and it is hoped that this trend will continue. Unfortunately, one comes across excessively marked pieces by some writers even today.

The Third Phase

Some blending of communicational and mechanical aspects should be undertaken in the third phase. In fact, what happens in this phase is the beginning and basis of what will continue, though in an expanding frame, through the rest of the teaching effort.

Some modalities of writing will be taken up the next chapter. The student will need to be progressively eased into expressional devices like punctuation side by side with his efforts to communicate in English. Eventually, that effort to communicate should be the dominant focus of the teacher. At the university level he will find young adults, some of whom have surprisingly well developed ideas in an Urdu or regional language expressional context.

The link between language and ideas mentioned in earlier chapters gets further confirmation in the observation of students. Idea generation does seem to depend on language. A student who thinks easily in Urdu will complain that he gets no ideas when he tries to write in English. It has already been suggested that the transference to a second language universe be done gradually, and that it does not matter if a lot that is obviously 'Urdu' shows up in the student's early efforts in English. He will become better as he progresses, if he begins to write: but he will hardly move if his initial output in English remains non-existent or insignificantly small.

Two pieces (A and B) are appended to show that progress is possible in a positive atmosphere. They were written by the student mentioned earlier in this chapter. Another example (C) is included for comparison. This was written by a female student as a piece of intrinsically motivated writing done in the classroom; no help was provided by the teacher. Generally, female writers write 'better' (in the sense of 'more correct') than male ones, though male writing sometimes seems more 'creative[3] and adventurous. This might reflect the greater social pressure on women for correct behaviour.

Chapter 8 Notes

1. 1 Williams, 129

2. Ibid.

3. Ibid., 130

4. The essentials of Kaplan's observations are discussed in Ibid., 159-160

5. Ibid., 159

6. Ibid., 160

7. Conrad, J. *Heart of Darkness.* Wordsworth Classics, 1995, 122-123

8. Legouis, E., and Cazamian. L.. *A History-of English Literature,* preface, vii

9. Ibid., 971

10. Ondatje, M, *Anil's Ghost.* Alfred Knopf NY, 2000, 190-191

11. Azam, I., *Literary' Studies: Theory and Creativity,*

12. PFI, Islamabad, 1999-2000,298

13. 12. Hemingway, E., *A Farewell to Anns,* Master Publishing

14. Lahore, 1999,28

15. 13. Sheridan, R., "The Art of Reading", *Works,* ed., Stainforth,

16. 1874, 97

17. 14. Stevenson, R., "Style in Literature: Its Technical Elements" in

18. Kleiser, G., *Practical English,* Funk and Wagnalls, NY and

19. London, 1929, Lesson 17,23

20. 15. Hilton, J., *Good-bye. Mr. Chips.* Oxford (Pakistan), 1999, 44-45

Chapter Nine
Teaching Writing to Senior Students

One comes across exhortations such as, *'(write)...clearly, appropriately and concisely'* (1), or, *'revise and rewrite... until your message comes across as clearly and effectively as possible'* (2), in book after book of writing instruction.

At what point can a second language learner still struggling with basics be confident that what he has written satisfies these criteria? Words like these rest very much on subjective judgement; what seems clear, concise and effective to the writer might not appear so to the reader. The problems are multiplied when there are many readers. It is suggested that no such restrictive criteria be imposed on the writing process in the early stages. At some stage the writer will have to consider his likely audience, but in the beginning let him write for himself.

Writing with the constant pressure of sounding clear and appropriate to others, when one is not even sure what sounds clear and appropriate to them, simply adds another layer of difficulty. The writer is already strongly inhibited by a fear that what he has written will be 'judged' by the reader. For the student the most important reader and judge is the teacher, or, if there is an external system of testing, the examiner. The judgement is usually based on the reader's own leanings or expectations. Judging new or relatively unknown things is done in terms of old, or relatively well known things. Yet every new piece of writing is a creation in a very real sense, even if it is not a world shaking piece of art. By rights every new piece should be judged by criteria implicit in it, and not in terms of what has gone before. However, as everybody knows, this rarely happens.

Nevertheless, this is what the teacher should strive for. It is difficult for him to distance himself from his own prejudices; but he should remember that what is given to him for evaluation belongs to the student. It emerges from the student's personality and represents the way he sees the world. The teacher should not expect the student to conform exactly, or even approximately, to the way he conceives things or writes himself. A lot of what can be described as the 'writing health' of students depends on the teacher's attitudes in this regard. One talks about encouraging creativity: the massive use of the red pencil coupled with the strict application of English conventions can do a lot to stifle it (3).

The direction of this thesis so far has been towards taking the senior student back to some basics, to engender writing and thinking maturity through certain exercises and approaches, to encourage the manipulation of language and to take another look at things like pointing, especially at the important marks, the full stop, the comma, the question mark and the capital letter. If one desires to write in English, a certain acceptance will have to be made of the conventions that have grown along with it, but not in an atmosphere of fear that deviations from those conventions will lead to failure or disgrace. It is a thin line. The thing should be English, but not so rigidly English that nothing gets written at all.

Each teacher will have to judge for himself how much his students need to be taken back to basics. Generally, no two classes will be the same, even at the same level. Generally, every student will be different from every other student. There is little point in forcing students who already know quite a lot through all the painful details again. If study time is to be used efficiently, they would benefit more from concentrating on areas of weakness than on areas of strength. This places a large burden on the teacher, who becomes responsible for all of his students, collectively and individually. It runs parallel with an equally onerous duty to judge how much each student needs, and to adjust various aspects of the course to suit that student. If student A seems to have a good grasp of, say, capital letters, why insist that he do yet more work in it? It goes without saying that the teacher will not be able to do this satisfactorily if the class is very large.

A pre-test might help. Most placement or entry tests are tests of writing, but they tend to have a strong grammar bias. It is easier for a teacher to see if the right form of the verb has been used, or if the blank space has been filled properly. The thing is either right or wrong. Some of these tests can be marked mechanically from templates or marking keys: Whatever be the value of multiple choice, sentence completion or true/false type questions, they have come to dominate testing procedures in the last twenty years or so. However, an ability to write cannot be assumed from them, even if a student gets a lot of these items right.

Some pre-tests also have items designed to reveal the student's skills at writing. These usually consist of asking the student to write a composition on a topic chosen from a short selection of topics. But this is precisely the 'end-product' approach that encourages some of the bad habits noted earlier. Some candidates for admission have an uncanny ability to seem better than they really are in such tests. When put to the real test in subsequent classroom or homework writing assignments, they tend to do relatively badly.

Homework assignments are usually done better than classroom ones. One obvious reason for this is that the student is not under a time-bound neurosis to perform in front of sniggering classmates, or, worse still, a disapproving teacher. He has more time to think about the topic. A less charitable explanation is that he gets help from other sources.

Class assignments are sometimes reduced to nothing as students sit fidgeting or staring at the walls. All the difficulties noted in earlier chapters rise to the surface during such assignments. Yet of all the ways suggested so far, they are the best for judging the present ability of students to write. This is where the teacher's patience and power to motivate his students are truly tested.

Vocabulary

In his 'process' approach, the teacher might need to start at the most obvious place, even with older students. That place is the word, the basic building block of language. It is not required of anyone, even of the professional writer, that he should know the meanings of all or half or even a fifth of the words available in the lexical repository of the English language (nobody, not even the most facile and scholarly of native speakers, comes anywhere near a total acquisition). The kind of work he is engaged in will provide some definition and boundaries for the type and number of words he will need to learn. Physics has its own range of words, as does geography or mathematics. The study of literature makes use of the widest vocabulary and has the most indistinct boundaries, as this field encroaches on several others. Even so, in gross numbers a student of literature could probably make do with an active vocabulary of two or three thousand words.

The passive vocabulary for literature would need to be larger, and usually is. The recognition vocabulary of the receptive skills is often several times the size of the practical vocabulary of the productive skills. A person recognises and understands a word when somebody else uses it, but might never or very rarely think of using it himself. In general receptive skills are more readily tapped than productive ones, although there is always some overlap. Milton used a vocabulary of about eleven thousand words for *Paradise Lost*. However, in writing about this epic a student might not need much more than two thousand.

Creativity, the undercurrent of this work, is not licence. Liberties may be taken with the language, but not to the extent of destroying its social framework. It is the vehicle for communication with other people, who will respond only if what is written is intelligible. Vocabulary exercises are best when words are used in context. One comes across perplexing malapropisms and spoonerisms in Pakistani English, a transference of sensibility produced by an essentially 'Urdu' yearning for the elevated and indirect style (4a).

> '..If his letter to the nation is anything to go by, he and his advisers are convinced that good, wholesome and lurid prose can still work wonders. Since the people are by and large idiots, a good rousing speech with dramatic imagery thrown in, will paper over whatever cracks are visible and keep the people from ever getting to see the real picture.

> "Be a witness, countrymen," apart from being grammatically wrong, is rightly translated from the original Urdu. It is difficult to imagine if the piece could have been written in English with the same "effect." Mr X's speech writers haven't changed, it is obvious. The same florid and theatrical style that used to be the hallmark of (his) speeches is very much in bloom...

> The purple letter goes on. It talks of "rank cruelty", "cold dungeon", "scepter (?) of solitary confinement"...

> Although Mr X declares that when he was in power, he "cared a fig for anyone in the world"—I still can't work that one out. Firstly, he was not into figs. Had he said, "fried sparrows' I would have bought it...'

Ornament and bombast are still the ideals of some writers in Pakistan. The author's reaction might be a little different from that of the author of this article, though his comments are apt. At least something has been written, and it is no great sin to write English in an Urdu way. However, at this level, the ghost writer should have been more careful. It is assumed that by 'scepter' he meant 'spectre'. Student writing needs to be low-key. It is representative rather than expressive for most of its purposes. The basic job of the student is to *inform* his teacher or examiner, not to *persuade* or *move* him in any way.

It is suggested that words be introduced in a contextual format, something like that shown in the example. An additional problem with the learning of words is that they can have many meanings in denotations, connotations and euphemisms. A word's denotations would need to be distinguished from its connotations. For example, the word 'run' has a basic denotative meaning of moving rapidly. But in a good dictionary this simple word will have about seventy entries, separately or in combination with prepositions, to form verbs; plus about thirty meanings as a noun; plus a fair number as an adjective, well over a hundred in all.

Sometimes the same word can have opposite meanings. *Cleave* can mean 'adhere closely', or 'cut down the middle'. *Sanction* as a verb means 'permit/authorise', and as a noun, 'restriction/punishment'. Sometimes opposite words can have the same meaning, especially in colloquial language; *fat* chance and *slim* chance both mean *hardly any chance at all*

This aspect of word usage adds another broad area of

caution and inhibition to English usage, another block to creativity. Yet it must be tackled by both the teacher and the student. Creativity is not total freedom. It achieves nothing if what is written offers no meaning to other users of the language. The game of tennis allows endless variations of length, height, pace and direction, but it is played within the regulatory functions of a net and guidelines marked on the ground.

Sample exercise:

a. *Dictionary entry*

Incendiary, *n.* 1. A person who maliciously sets fire to property; 2. One guilty of arson; 3 one who inflames factions; 4 a firebrand; 5. A bomb dropped from an aeroplane and intended to cause a fire

  i. A thousand incendiaries rained down on the city, but this was not a cooling rain (meaning number_____)

  ii. Mr Smith's house was set on fire last night. The owner of the house next door is thought to be the incendiary, as he is known to have quarreled with Mr Smith (meaning number_____)

(*Note*: there should be no hesitation about (i). The incendiaries here are *bombs* (meaning number 5), although the idea of hot rain is awkward. The second statement might cause trouble. The difference in meaning between entries

1, 2 and 4 in this dictionary is small. However, the context indicates incendiarism confined to a single malicious act, rather than habitual or criminal incendiarism, so the best choice would be meaning number 1.)

Word building is useful in that it helps the student to work out meanings for himself. Learning common prefixes and suffixes and seeing how their application to word roots and bases can generate new words and meanings, is a satisfying exercise that has lasting effects on the student. It is strongly recommended.

Synonyms

One of the advantages of the language is the large number of synonyms offered by its vocabulary. English may not be the equal of some other languages in this regard (Arabic is often quoted as being particularly rich), but it has a lot of variety. Strictly speaking, perfect synonyms are rare. In most cases they represent the same idea, but in a slightly different context. The study of groups of words described as synonyms is important for developing precision of expression. It also helps in expressing thought in a variety of ways.

A mistake made by some Pakistani students is to think that one word may substitute exactly for another. Another mistake is to think that if two words are not exact substitutes, they must represent different ideas. These mistakes grow from the expectation of absolutes, whereas the truth lies somewhere in between. The sense does not coincide precisely; often two words will look at the same thing from slightly different perspectives.

Synonyms are useful not only for substitution but for bridging operations between one idea and another, the alternative word partaking of some meaning in this context and some in the other.

The words 'infer' and 'prove' might illustrate this point. Some overlapping exists in the action of these verbs, but the direction in either case is different. 'Inferring' moves from premises to conclusions, while 'proving' moves from conclusions to premises. Likewise, Aristotle informs us that 'pity' and 'fear' are really two sides of the same coin, i.e., that we pity in others what we fear for ourselves.

The fact that many ordinary words can have a large number of meanings creates difficulties in deciding applications. An example is given from the word 'plain'. It is possible to substitute *plain* for *intelligible* in the following sentence without much distortion of meaning:

Please give me an *intelligible* answer.

It is also possible to substitute *plain* for *homely* in the following:

Her features are rather *homely*.

However, trying to straddle the divide through the common mediation of 'plain' would produce strange utterances, 'Please give me a *homely* answer', or, 'Her features are rather *intelligible*".

Thus, a common way of 'opening' (beginning) a meeting in Pakistan is 'inaugurating' it, an unnecessary striving for the effect of a high style; though it is quite acceptable to 'inaugurate' (instal) a new leader in the country. The *thesaurus* concept of providing lists of synonyms and antonyms has had a mixed effect on writing. For example, in recent writing in journalism, the desire to produce something different from the ordinary has resulted in a progressive shift in the word 'change'. This began as 'metamorphose', then became 'metamorph', and now sometimes appears as 'morph', which means 'form' rather than 'change'. The idea of change lies in the 'meta' part of this word, but this has been erroneously dropped. Straining for effect can lead to strange usage.

Prudence is required in the learning and application of synonyms.

Sentence Manipulation

The sentence is the basic unit of language. Its rhetoric, once mastered, opens doors to larger units of writing. The student who has grasped the rhetorical relationships between the subject and predicate and other elements that may be added, is well poised to understand the rhetorical relationships of larger units of expression.

It would be presumptuous to dismiss what has taken place since Chomsky as old wine in new bottles, or as modern, pseudo-scientific, jargonistic ways of describing the obvious. However, some of the older approaches had something in common with those we find today. The old schoolroom activity of parsing sentences had many of the same elements. It was an unpopular activity, and probably a waste of time, though its proponents defended it stoutly. When a student could already use the language in meaningful situations, there was little point in asking him to analyse it. And if he could not use it, analysing it probably did little to help him understand it. The researcher's direct experience with Pakistani and other nonnative students leads him to believe that T-G grammar in its current presentation is not particularly helpful.

The proof of this particular grammatical pudding is in the linguistic eating. Very little visible gain in understanding or forming language has been observed from the teaching of diagrams (see chapter two; even the most rudimentary of sequences can lead to a dauntingly complex set of possibilities), or the application of transformation rules (which, as mentioned earlier, are plausible but not demonstrable). On the other hand, confusion and misapplication have sometimes been observed.

Brackets can become overwhelming, even in simple utterances. A fully designed tree diagram does not look like a proper utterance in any language. And the demonstration of transformations for the formation of (for example) a question from a roughly formed kernel structure does little to help when the student can form a question already. Quasi-mathematical abstractions contribute little in the quantification, qualification or clarification of things when the concrete is already available in the form of the language. Why not go straight to the language?

Asking students to try out as many ways as possible of saying something seems more effective in touching the idea of transformation. Quite a lot can be done with simple statements. Students think round structures and dip into their own reservoir of language for parallel words and structures:

a. English is the most widely used language in the world today

b. No other language is used as widely as English in the world today

c. English is used more widely than any other language in the world today

d. The most widely used language in the modern world is English

e. You will not find any language more widely used today than English

f. Of all languages, English is the most widely used in the modem world

g. Nowadays, English is used in more parts of the world than any other language

h. No language has the geographical spread of English

This does not exhaust the possibilities. Some statements are clumsy, but they all serve to convey the same idea.

Deviant Usage

The author has come across awkward usage time and again. A quick survey of Pakistani English was made in chapter three. In that chapter, deviations arising mainly through first language interference were discussed. However, another class of deviations exists which seem to rise from the second language learner's imperfect resolution of ambiguous areas in the language itself. Pakistanis would probably share such deviations, or some of them, with other second language learners. They occur frequently enough to suggest widespread misapplications.

1. In arranging sentences, words that are in some kind of relationship should be placed as close to each other as possible;
   a. *His son works in a factory, who is a welder*
   b. His son, who is a welder, works in a factory

2. When two nouns are connected by *and,* the plural form of the verb should be used (Urdu uses the singular verb in the gender of the last noun in the series, but this might not be the cause of this particular variation in Pakistan. Other non-native speakers sometimes make mistakes here, and so do some native speakers)
   a. *Money and fame is what men desire*
   b. Money and fame are what men desire

3. When two singular nouns are connected by *or* or *nor,* the singular form of the verb should be used:
   a. *(Either) This table or that one are suitable for the job*

b. (Either) This table or that one *is* suitable for the job

However, some relaxation is visible in this practice. Also, the old recommendation that *either/or* and *neither/nor* should apply to no more than two items is no longer followed.

4. If the nouns are in the plural, the verb should follow suit:
   a. *Neither these tables nor those ones is suitable for the job*
   b. Neither these tables nor those ones are suitable for the job
5. If the nouns are mixed in number or type, the verb should follow the nearest noun:
   a. Neither the king nor the people *are* ready for change
   b. Either you or I *am* wrong
   c. The news *is* not very good
   d. Ten years *is* a long time to wait for results
   e. The lord and master *is* waiting for you

In b, some people would prefer to say, "Either you are, or I am, wrong', but this is unnecessary. In c, the noun *news* is singular, although it looks plural. In d, *a span of time* has been totalled into a singular concept. In e, both nouns refer to the *same* thing, so the singular form of the verb is used.

6. Confusion is sometimes seen in determining the primary noun when other ideas are appended:

   a. The teacher, together with her students, *is* feeling tired

   b. The laboratory, with all its equipment, *was* destroyed

   c. The trees, in conjunction with the telephone wire, *were* damaged in the storm

   d. Nothing *pleases* so much as good words in the right place

7. Adjective pronouns sometimes cause trouble. Should it be (a) 'these kind of problems', (b)'this kind of problems', or (c) 'this kind of problem'? If the problems fall into a single class, 'this' is preferable (b). Also, whether one is talking about one problem or many, it is usually enough to say 'problem', because a singular class of plurals can supply a plural concept if required (c). Idiomatic usage might accept 'these' also (a), leapfrogging the singularity of 'kind' to the plurality of 'problems'. For students in a formal course of education, formal usage is preferable.

8. The placement of limiters can affect meaning:

   a. He is *only* trying to do his job

honestly

b.   *Only* he is trying to do his job honestly

c.   He is trying to do *only* his job honestly

(or)

d.   Aslam has *just* finished his work

e.   *Just* Aslam has finished his work

9.   Faults are sometimes seen with the verb following *each, every, either,* and *neither.* The singular form is required, regardless of the way nouns are stacked:

a.   Each chair and table *was* painted brown

b.   Every one of the children *was* asked to sing

c.   Either of you is eligible for the job

d.   Neither of these candidates *is* eligible

10. Corresponding conjunctions are often used faultily:

a.   *Though* may be followed by *yet* or *nevertheless*

b. *Whether*   *or*

c.. *Either*   *or*

d.. *Neither*   *nor*

e.. *As*   *as*

f.*As*   *so*

g. *So*   *as*

h. *So*   *that*

    i. *Both*   *and*
    j. *Not only*   *but also*

10. The placement of words like *also, rather* and *even* can affect meaning:
    a. He *also* tries to teach his son (in addition to something else)
    b. He tries to teach his son *also* (in addition to someone else)

    a. The dress suits you *rather* than her
    b. The dress *rather* suits you

    a. *Even* in the speech of famous men you will discover errors
    b. In the speech *even* of famous men you will discover errors

11. *Further* is used for abstract things, *farther* for distance

    a. Have you anything *further* to say?
    b. The bridge *farther* down the river is under water

The purpose here is not to give an exhaustive list of corrections, but to stimulate some interest in usage.

Rhetoric

The term is used today in the context of language control for the purpose of persuading others:

    ...What we currently know about language

suggests that we use it to perform actions. One factor that distinguishes good writers from poor ones is their awareness that their writing, if successful, will produce an effect on those who read it. This, then, is what rhetoric is about: bringing about a change in an audience. Considering that accomplishing this goal requires knowledge of subject and audience, of sociology and psychology, it seems unlikely that a writer who understands the rhetoric of writing—and it need not be explicit understanding—can produce an essay without learning something... (5)

A lot of writing activity in the classroom (or as home assignments) is falsely purposeful in that the purpose is simply to complete a given assignment, not to plan language with goals and intentions. It is difficult to understand the intention of the teacher in such assignments, and lacking one of his own, the student produces a set of words on paper. The completion of the assignment becomes the purpose of the piece:

> ... But meaning requires intention. Without an intention, composing is meaningful only inasmuch as the act of putting words down on paper becomes the purpose of the writing task, which isn't meaningful at all. It results in merely simple representation, realized through the act of putting words on a piece of paper. This is not a rhetorical act... (6)

One fundamental difference in writing and speaking is often overlooked:

> ... As soon as one *decides* to write, one has formulated an intention based on the logical properties of the act. We can understand this concept better if we consider that writing, unlike speech, always has an intentional object. Thus when one decides to write, the conditions of satisfaction specify not only the requirement (that one write) but the thing required (that one write *something*). Therefore, one decides to write a letter or a journal or a report or a shopping list or an essay... ...We cannot make the same claim for utterances. Individual utterances obviously have objects in the sense that they are ' *about* something, and they share this characteristic with individual written expressions, but "speaking about something" is not the same as "speaking something". One case is not intentional, whereas the other is. Note in this regard that we cannot say, ʿi have decided to speak a letter," or " I have decided to speak a shopping list"...(7)

This proposition needs to be tested further. Its implication is that the inner and outer mechanisms that decide language understand and follow 'reality' in some way, although, if this idea is accepted, the phenomenon of change in language at a structural level becomes rather difficult to comprehend, unless reality keeps on changing. Why should English, for example, have dropped gender and inflections when they were doing the job of reflecting reality (whatever reality was at that point) satisfactorily? And if reality changed at that point to something else, something that required a non-inflectional, rigid 'word order' way, rather than a flexible, inflectional way, of expressing things, why did it not change equally for so many other languages, languages that have not seen fit to drop gender and inflections?

Williams suggests that human beings use the verbs 'speak' and 'write' differently because, in their inner language categories and structures, there is an unconscious recognition that the modes of expression are different from each other.

Substituting 'talk' for 'speak', one finds immediate confirmation; one cannot say, 'I will talk a lesson', although one can say, "I will talk *about* a lesson'. (In informal speech, Americans sometimes say 'He's *talking* big money here,' where 'talk' is used in the sense of 'discuss').

Substituting 'say' for 'speak' changes the formation, but not the implications. 'Say' works more like 'write' than 'speak' does, e.g. "1 will say *something* about this house'— one cannot say 'I will say about the house'. Actually, 'say' is not a satisfactory substitute for 'speak'. One can say things in writing as well, but one cannot usually speak things in writing. Likewise, other possible substitutes such as 'discuss', 'announce', 'aver', 'assert', 'state', etc., really work in different categories of comprehension.

Substituting 'pen' for 'write' gives much the same inherent language differentiation, "I will pen a lesson,' but not, "1 will pen *about* a lesson'. However, synonymous verbs are not exact substitutes. 'Write' permits writing *about* something in apparently the same way as speaking, except that it is not really the same way. The real meaning of 'I will write about a lesson' is '1 will write (a paragraph or essay or tract) about a lesson.'

Does a parallel differentiation exist in Urdu? 'Main boloonga' (I will speak) and 'main likhoonga' (1 will write) do not show any linguistic differentiation in the bare statement, any more than 'I will speak' or 'I will write' do in English. However, the implications are similar to those of the English verbs. When one says 'main ghar ke baare main likhoonga,' (I will write about the house), the implication is that some form of written expression (an essay or a letter) will be created in order to discuss the house.

But does not 'I will speak about the house' imply that some sort of spoken expression will be used to discuss the house? If there is a difference, it is because spoken language disappears in a puff of air, whereas written language stays as a concrete record. Confirmation of Williams' general prooposition comes in Urdu parallels, as in, 'main khat likhoonga' (I will write a letter), but not 'main takrir boloonga' (1 will speak a speech), which would be rendered more like 'main takrir karoonga', (1 will do a speech). The parallels are not exact, indicating some points of divergence in the two languages. And of course, 'dictating' is not the same as speaking, just as 'reading aloud' is not the same as speaking.

One sees other instances of how English employs different verbs in different ways, especially when one action is followed by another. Some are followed by gerunds ('he admitted *taking* the money'), some by *to infinitives* ('I want *to know* who did this'), some by either the *gerund* or the *to infinitive* ('this wall needs *painting'* / 'this wall needs *to be painted'*), some by the simple infinitive ('please let me finish my work') and some by either the *simple* or the *to* infinitive ('he helped me *finish* my work' / 'he helped me *to finish* my work'.

At the back of this apparent disorder is an unconscious or subconscious recognition that some verbs are attitudinal, some causative, some receptive by implication, some multifunctional, and some purposeful. There are psychological reasons for a language's variations in usage, although these can only be hinted at. Likewise, there are reasons why two verbs for the productive use of language in different conventions, 'write' and 'speak', are used in different ways.

The thrust of these observations is that the writing of second language students often displays a confusion of act with content. They begin to believe that the writing is the doing.

It is not so much that a writer *does* use certain rhetorical devices as it is *why* he does so. Of course, he may do so consciously and calculatedly, to produce certain effects in accordance with his intentions. Conscious stylists such as Hemingway, Bacon or Lyly undoubtedly exist, and their kind of writing has a certain appeal to some people. However, a lot of what happens in writing is unconscious, and an awareness of underlying mental processes might be useful, even if one cannot count or describe them exactly.

It is not possible to pry into the workings of the mind, but certain plausible assumptions may be made. The human infant must have an innate awareness of *time* and *space,* reinforced by the periodicity of its own hunger pangs, perhaps, for time, and a consciousness of its mother's coming closer and moving away, for space. *Rhythms* large and small soon define its living patterns. Likewise, it must have some capacity to form *associations;* it not only recognises its own mother quickly, it begins to observe things together in relationships, either *causal,* or *sequential,* or *spatial.* It soon learns that doing something produces something else. It cries, and gets attention. An appreciation of causality, if it is not innate, is soon developed. The assumption that the infant brain is also able to establish relationships in wholes to parts *{analysis)* or in parts to wholes *(synthesis)* is a reasonable one to make, because these processes are basic to the understanding of things. It is also most likely that a good deal of *comparing, contrasting* and *classifying* goes on. Without these, and probably other, basic categories of ability and comprehension, not much by way of a meaningful acquisition of knowledge could even begin to take place. Yet babies observe and learn a great deal about the world, whether they are taught or not.

The teacher should base his teaching approaches on an awareness of these factors and exploit whatever writing skills are already available for (a) providing a pathway to writing in English, and (b) strengthening that writing through rhetorical principles. Some of these factors will be examined in chapter nine.

Chapter 9 Notes

1. Burton, S., *Practical Writing,* Macmillan, 1987,

2. Bovee, C, and Thill, J., *Business Communication Today,* Mcgraw-Hill, NY, 1995, 104

3. See report entitled "SPELT session emphasises creative writing in children", *The News,* 20 September, 2000.

4. The speaker on this occasion was Ms Rukhsana Saeed. She was quoted as saying, ' Just guide them with the minimum of red ink. It is not the grammar or punctuation, but the ideas that matter in primary classes...'. This is largely the approach adopted by the author for senior students as well. Grammar and punctuation do matter for senior classes, but they should not be the deciding factor in a student's efforts.

5. Names have been removed from the excerpts: (Hassan, M., "Get Real", *The News,* 18 October 2000. This is a commentary on a letter released to the press by a politician)

6. Williams, 48

7. Ibid., 34

8. Ibid., 41

Chapter Ten
Models for Analysis

Copying or analysing the works of others does not seem to improve one's writing ability significantly. Till recently, reading was considered to be the prime source of writing. In fact, studying (including writing) was, and still is in some circles, considered to be synonymous with reading. One still goes to some universities to 'read', as though this is the dominant activity and all others derivative and secondary. This is reinforced by an unfortunate parallel in Urdu: the word 'parhai' is commonly used for reading and studying.

There is a clear causal relationship between reading and writing in the early years. A school child would need to be able to recognise letters and words before he could begin to write them. It is possible, also, that learning to write improves reading competence in children, indicating causality in both directions. However, at some stage the connections become weaker. Continuing with the tennis analogy introduced before, practising the forehand does not automatically result in an ability to hit a backhand, although both sides are linked through the general mental and physical abilities of the same person. As with all the skills of language, so also with reading and writing—some areas mesh, and some remain free.

Till the end of the nineteen sixties, books like *A Reading Guide to Belter Writing,* Cox, M, (Chandler, San Francisco, 1968), *Reader and Writer,* Harford and Vincent (Houghton Mifflin, Boston, 1954), *A Reading Approach to College Writing* (SRA, Illinois, 1967), or *Prose for Senior Students,* Gill and Newell (Macmillan, Toronto, 1951) were common. Even in the nineteen eighties, analysts like Krashen (see chapter one) continued to support the link. The supposedly self-evident truth that exposing a student to good examples of English in reading texts would help him to write better was rarely questioned, and lay behind a lot of drudgery in literature, often with disappointing results. That the results of this approach in Pakistan are more often disappointing than not is known to every university teacher. Writing has to be handled in its own right, not treated as a corollary of reading.

Nevertheless, provided a person continues to practise his writing, reading can help to make him a 'full' man, full of possibilities and ideas culled from the experience of others and filtered through the complexities of his own experience and psychology. Provided he has also done something for his writing skills, he can move some of that fullness over to them as well. Perhaps something of another person's style and language can also be acquired, though the idiosyncrasies of each person will largely determine the way he expresses himself. And differences of approach, comprehension, style and expression are much more in evidence when there are basic cultural differences. Regardless of how well he writes in English, a Pakistani cannot, and should not try to, conceal his identity under this language. Far better than trying to copy either matter or style is to use reading as a means of stimulating ideas. Good reading is an active process, not an effort at total recall. People who try to commit passages to memory use their reading skills in a wrong way. It is a continuation of the belief that utterances have to be learnt by heart, and that this will give the reader competence in the language. As one writing course has it:

> ...to accentuate the dynamic, interactive character of the writing process [we] begin by encouraging students to consider how dialogue empowers writers to engage readers...From here we turn to... ways writers make sense of texts for themselves and others through writing. We invite writers to explore how writing aids reading and how writing flows naturally from it. We provide opportunities here for students to do three kinds of writing: (a)writing to understand texts; (b) writing to explain texts; and (c) writing to evaluate texts. (1)

A few writers have been able to convincingly adjust their style according to their subject, but not many. Disputatious Adam and Eve, for example, sound quite similar to each other (both sound like Milton) in *Paradise Lost*, as do Rosalind and Orlando in *As You Like It*, although the reputations of the authors of these works are overwhelming. Keats, trying the sustained high style for an epic in the nineteenth century, soon abandoned the effort. It did not come easily to him.

As mentioned in chapter eight, the primary step in composing a piece of writing, short or long, is insight into the rhetoric of the sentence. Once this is achieved, larger units become manageable:

> To say that we teach someone to write is perhaps a figure of speech. In actuality, what we call 'writing' is a synthesis of many kinds of experience, operating, obviously, through the innate ability of the writer. These experiences are acquired in school, in daily living, and, above all, in the mental processes of the writer. Rather than saying we teach someone to write, it is safer to say that we encourage writing by providing the occasion to write, by providing critical aid to the writer, and by teaching him certain skills whose advancement and progress enable him to grow in power to communicate. (2)

These authors go on to say:

> These 'skills' are four in number:

> 1. The skill *of sentence patterns.* Founded on a few basic patterns, English prose construction offers an almost infinite variety of sentence forms. Growth in skill and discrimination in the use of sentence patterns is the means to

increasing success in the conversion of ideas to written expression.

2. The skill *of unity, coherence, and development.* This involves a maturing in the ability to deal with one topic, or idea, from a few words to an extended thesis, and to subordinate details to a single emphasis, a 'centeredness' of composition.

3. The skill of *organization.* Closely related to unity, coherence and development, *organization* provides the means to know where and how to start a communication, what to emphasize and subordinate, how much to include, how to arrange the material, and how to bring communication to a satisfactory conclusion. It is the skill of *orderliness.*

4. The skill *of diction.* This skill involves two learning processes: the acquisition of words with increasing depth of meanings, and the discriminating selection of words in prose construction to achieve clarity of meaning, exactness of tone and intent, and individuality of style. (3)

The author's reaction to such classifications is that they tend to be simplistic. Probably a great deal more goes on in good writing than can be reduced to four categories like this. However, it is useful for students to have the essentials isolated in this manner. At some stage they might be able to rise above them. The concern of this short work is less with good writing than with adequate writing. Nevertheless, the ideas outlined above represent the irreducible, especially in regard to sentences.

The basic sentence with its subject-predicate format can be manipulated in a number of ways. Different kinds of sentences are described as follows:

1. *Simple:* this has only one subject and one predicate, regardless of its length:
    a. He plays tennis
    b. That poor man, pitied by everyone, died last week
    c. A writer's first job is to satisfy himself

2. *Compound:* when two simple sentences or two principal clauses are connected, usually with conjunctions like *and, but* or *hence,* or substitutes of such conjunctions (also, besides, moreover/ however, nevertheless, whereas/accordingly, so, therefore, etc), a compound sentence is formed:
    a. Youth passes quickly, so make the best of it.
    b. Summer is upon us, and the water table has fallen
    c. Writing seems to be difficult, but it is a powerful tool for communication

3. *Complex:* when a sentence contains one or more principal and one or more subordinate clauses, it is said to be complex:
    a. The painting he has done on this wall is very interesting
    b. The fact that writing is complex makes it difficult to master

4. *Balanced:* When two clauses of similar form are used for expressing a parallel or contrasted meaning, the sentence thus constructed is said to be balanced:
    a. Man proposes: God disposes
    b. Reading maketh a lull man; speaking, a ready man; and writing, an exact man

5. *Periodic:* In this the main statement is delayed till the end of the sentence. However, it should be controlled from the beginning. Such sentences are often introduced with a conditional element:
    a. If this motion is introduced, if it is approved by both houses, and if it wins the general acceptance of the populace, God willing, it will make a large contribution to poverty reduction in the country
    b. Unless the party can show its credentials in a better light, 1 shall not support it

    c. I know he gave you his word, but how reliable is an unwritten assurance?

6.   *Loose:* when clauses and phrases are added in an apparently disorganised manner, almost as afterthoughts, the result is an informal, conversational tone:

    a. There is something repellant, almost dead, like an artificial flower, no matter how carefully crafted, about an overworked sentence—with all its imperfections the living flower is, I say again, much better than the perfect artifact

7.   *Long/Short: B*ecause Urdu has a loose pointing system, Pakistani writers tend to produce endless, rambling sentences in English through a series of coordinated statements using 'ands' and 'buts' long after the principal statement has exhausted itself. Long sentences are not bad in and of themselves, and may be used sometimes to give dignity and weight to the discourse. However, brevity is a virtue to be cultivated most of the time, as it helps understanding. Short, Hemingway-type sentences are easy to comprehend, though they, too, can be overused. A judicious mixture of short and long is probably the most

interesting to read:

a. (long) Never let it be said again, as some people have said in the past, that the leaders of this sorely tried nation did not rise to the occasion, such as this dire one, with a great and powerful enemy threatening our eastern borders, and a carrion vulture balefully poised in the north, too weak to attack us should we live through the coming contest, yet waiting, waiting, to feed on the remains, should we perish in the deadly struggle

b. (short) Some people prefer to write short poems

8. *Interrogative:* questions are not always questions. The question form is sometimes used for emphasis:

   a.   What is the leader's job if it isn't to lead the nation?

   b.   Why does it rain whenever we want to play outside?

9. *Exclamatory:* to be used sparingly:

   a.   What a beautiful morning!

   b.   Just look at that stupid man!

10. *Optative/Subjunctive:* a wish is expressed in such sentences:

    a.   God be with you

      b.   May all your dreams come true

11. *Imperative:* direct instructions or orders are given in such sentences:
    a.   Shut that door
    b.   Mix the powder with the milk, then put the mixture on a low fire and stir until it thickens

In summary, *short* sentences give power and clarity, *long* ones give weight and dignity, *periodic* sentences create anticipation and interest, *balanced* sentences give harmony and contrast, and *loose* sentences make for an easy speaking style. One is diffident about suggesting a formula for senior students. However, in general the recommendation is for short, direct sentences most of the time, and for most assignments and subjects. However, other kinds of sentences may also be used if the topic or occasion seems to demand them.

A few do's and don't's are suggested here:

1. The subject should be sufficient to support the language—too often the student writer has little to say and hides the fact in a mass of words. It is better that a strong body be dressed simply than that a weak body be expanded artificially with frills and flounces. However, if the body is weak, something might usefully be done to fill it out

2. Limiters like 'only' and 'just' should be placed next to the words they qualify

3. Emphatic words should be placed in emphatic positions

4. Unlike speaking, which is hurried and poorly planned (although there is some short-phased, rapid planning here as well), writing is conducive to careful planning. This, with its unlimited capacity for revision, is its great strength, which gives it so many advantages over speaking. Pre-planning helps in the process of writing. However, it is possible to overdo it, to the extent that the living, spontaneous element of language is lost. Writing should not be deadened by excessive advance outlining and structuring. Thought processes tend to develop from what is being said as much as, or more than, from pre-planning. Modem writing courses tend to make a fetish of *process,* as though this, too, needs to be bureaucratised; in other words, that step one *must* be completed before undertaking step two; writing an essay *cannot begin* until controlled, guided or free sessions of generating ideas have been completed. Not so. The human brain is a vaulting, self-exploring, self-motivating thing about which little is known, especially its vast underground of activity. Writing does not always need sessions of *brainstorming* before it can begin. Sometimes the very act of beginning reveals directions. Thoughts grow out of thoughts.

    However, much as one would like to justify the avoidance of restrictions, idea generation and creativity rest on a substratum of discipline and self-training in core skills. Azam identifies the essay as the core form in writing:

> '1 am personally of (he well-considered view that if you have mastered the art and skill of essay writing, you are on the way to creativity as a creative writer. For expertise in essay writing is the core and crux of creativity... '(4).

This view should be considered carefully. Not many writers writing in their *first* language can have equalled this writer's literary output in a *second* language.

5. Revision is important for self-correction and for useful additional inputs. However, excessive revision might be undesirable. This, too, can kill the original ideas. Second, third or fourth thoughts are not necessarily better than first ones.

6. Care should be taken with the idea of *unity*, both within a sentence and over the whole extent of the writing. It is this that informs paragraph construction and overall planning in the English convention, so that items clustered properly together move in a recognisable progression from a beginning, through a middle to an end. Sudden and frequent shifts of scene are disturbing, as are sudden shifts of tense and time. Too many heterogeneous ideas crowded into a narrow frame can make for bad reading. Too many interpolations and interruptions can

do the same. And the piece of writing should be finished when it is done.

The Rhetoric of Writing

As mentioned in chapter eight, rhetoric in the modern sense is not quite the same as it was in olden times, when it referred to effective oratory or persuasive writing. Then, it was customary to teach figures of rhetoric to make apprentice demagogues and writers aware of what could be done to raise their language to a level where it could affect other people in a desired way. Now it refers more to processes underlying an author's intention (see chapter eight, especially Willams' arguments).

Lists of some of the old figures can still be found in many writing courses, though it is questionable what the authors who introduce them into their courses hope to achieve by them. They are useful more for analysing other people's writing than for deliberate application. It is a rare writer who will consciously *decide* to use *synecdoches,* for example, at certain points in his writing. If such figures appear in an author's writing, it is more likely that subterranean communicational pressures have found their surface expression in them.

No list will be offered here. The empirical approach to psychology is behavioural, which means that very little can be hazarded about the inner working of the brain. The following statements are conjectural, since nothing can be done at this stage in human development to prove or disprove them. Some figures, like the simile and metaphor, are common, and are used frequently by people in ordinary communication. The underlying linguistic and mental activities behind the production of such figures can be sensed, even if they cannot be described accurately. *Comparing* and *contrasting* things has a lot to do with figures like the simile, the metaphor, the metonymy, humour and irony. *Analysing* and *synthesizing* things lie behind figures like the synecdoche. *Associating* things can be inferred behind personification and allegory. *Importance, emphasis, an inner anxiety* that salient points be driven home, stimulate devices like the hyperbole, the exclamation, the apostrophe, repetition, perhaps even climax.

The major goals in communication are said to be (a) to inform, (b) to persuade, (c) to convince, and (d) to entertain (3). *Information* might contain elements of instruction as well. *Persuasion* is seen as affecting a reader and moving him to act in a desired manner. *Convincing* a reader is more intellectual in that it tries to secure agreement rather than stimulate action. *Entertainment* has at its primary aim the pleasure a reader might get from what is written. One, some or all of these purposes arc used by writers, separately or in combination, usually under the mantle of one dominant purpose for any given assignment.

For the achievement of these purposes, attention has to be paid to several things. There is not much point in writing if it does not achieve, at least partially, what it sets out to do. A close look at factors like unity and coherence must be made, and some sort of planning, whether mental or written, is crucial in the process. Analysing the levels and needs of likely readers helps in establishing registers and degrees of formality. The question of diction, or style, is certainly of great importance. Its appropriacy is a prime factor in the success of the piece.

Analysing Pieces of Writing

While the output of this exercise in helping the process of writing is not established, it is a useful task to give, and one in which the teacher can participate extensively, provided he does not let his participation dominate the student's efforts. Once the student has begun to see what happens in effective writing, he will often continue to penetrate it to surprising levels. It is hoped, though one cannot be sure, that some of these insights will be transferred to the student's own writing.

Some samples follow:

I

Text A

"Now, the first merit which attracts the pages of a good writer, or the talk of a brilliant conversationalist, is the apt choice and contrast of the words employed. It is, indeed, a strange art to take these blocks, rudely conceived for the market or the bar, and by tact and application touch them to the finest meanings and distinctions, restore them to their primal energy, wittily shift them to another issue, or make them a drum to rouse the passions. But though this form of merit is, without doubt, the most sensible and seizing, it is far from being equally present in all writers. The effect of words in Shakespeare, their singular justice, significance, and poetic charm, is different, indeed, from the effect of words in Addison or Fielding. Or to take an example nearer home, the words in Carlyle seem electrified into an energy of lineament, like the faces of men furiously moved: while the

words in Macaulay, apt enough to convey his meaning, yet glide from the memory like undistinguished elements in a general effect. But the first class of writers have no monopoly on liter-ary merit. There is a sense in which Addison is superior to Carlyle; a sense in which Cicero is better than Tacitus; in which Voltaire exceeds Montaigne; it certainly lies not in the choice of words; it lies not in the interest of value or matter; it lies not in the force of intellect, of poetry, or of humour. The first three are hut infants to the second three; and yet each, in a particular point of literary art, excels his superior in the whole. What is that point? "

Text B

"It is an artful piece, that piece by Stevenson. No doubt those rolling, deep breathing clauses, each one fashioned exactly, first fixed with suitable mortar to other parts and then fitted into the whole, would have attracted the favourable attention of his contemporaries. While commenting on style, it is itself an exemplar of style, of the care with which the top writers of every generation have lovingly oiled and honed the tools of their craft.

His question at the end is singular. The answer, alas, is that all the carving and polishing in the world may not make a chair more comfortable, or more useful, than one hewn carelessly out of a few bits of wood. It may not make it more beautiful. Just as a fat man will find little comfort and therefore little beauty in a small though exquisitely finished chair, so each man will judge comfort, usefulness or beauty for himself.

'Aye, there's the rub,' as Shakespeare might say. This business of style is judged by people other than the writer, and each will judge it differently. For some, beauty lies in

utility or simplicity; for others, in adornment; for yet others, in harmony or in the 'speaking tones' of a written piece. I have friends, learned, sophisticated men and women, who are too impatient to read Stevenson, or indeed Lamb, Steele or Addison, or any of those others mentioned by Stevenson. They find the interests old-fashioned, the language contrived and irksome, the humour unfunny. Lawrence had the sense to see that literature, even great literature, rarely carries much meaning across the confines of its own time.

The answer to Stevenson's question is summed up in the word, 'sincerity.' Sincerity and honesty must take precedence over art. There is a point beyond which 'art' becomes self-defeating, especially when it loses sight of its basic purpose. Tastes have changed since Stevenson's time. They will go on changing. What seems forceful and effective to us today might seem banal and frivolous tomorrow. There are no universal elements of style beyond saying something simply and saying it so that your contemporaries can understand you. "

Questions:

1. Compare the style of the two texts.
2. Think of a piece of writing (in any language) which either pleases or displeases you because of its style. Give reasons for your reaction.

II

Texts A to D contain reports of an accident:

Q. Compare and contrast them, commenting on

interesting language features and on the way the report writers react to the same event:

A. Train Collides with Bus

Last night the driver of a slow, poorly lit, overloaded goods train was unable to stop in time when he saw a bus standing athwart his line at the unmanned Mill Hill crossing. His engine rammed into the bus, carrying it forward half a furlong. The driver almost lost consciousness when his head struck violently against the panel, but he remembers trying desperately to brake his lumbering train. Seven people in the bus died, including its driver. Eleven more were taken to hospital for injuries ranging from minor to severe. One middle-aged man is still lying in a coma with head injuries. Locals say that despite complaints nothing has been done to improve the safety of the crossing.

B. Disaster at Mill Hill

An accident waiting to happen. It needed just one dozy driver, or one motor flooding and stalling at the wrong time. The 6-Up freighter crashed into a bus at 7 yesterday evening, reduced it to ribbons of steel sheeting, and killed the driver and six of the passengers immediately. The final toll might rise in coming days, as some of the passengers are seriously hurt. One orderly at the hospital said, We all saw this coming. God knows how many times we \e asked for proper gates at the crossing. They might wake up now...

C. Speeding Train Trashes Bus: Seven Die

Mill Hill, January 27. A fast goods train slammed into a bus at the local crossing. The twisted body of the bus can be seen half a kilometer away from the point of impact. That proves how fast the train was running, say eye-witnesses. Nothing has happened for years, it's a perfectly safe crossing, say the authorities. The train driver was apparently drunk, reeling around and mumbling incoherently when rescuers got to the scene. Nothing could be done for the seven people sitting in the front two rows of the mangled bus, but the remaining passengers are said to be all right.

D. How Many More of These!

That was war-zone carnage at Mill Hill last night Seven precious lives were lost and several passengers were injured in a horrifying collision at the railway crossing. You could blame the bus driver, but the poor fellow's gone. You could blame the train driver, but the distraught man tried his best. You can't pull those dinosaurs up quickly, no matter how hard you bash away at the brakes. The blame rests squarely on those who are unwilling to put up gates or appoint people to look after these murderous crossings, cutting corners to save a few pennies. The real criminals are the smug bureaucrats. This is murder by negligence and we demand a proper accounting. And for the love of God do something before it happens again.

III

Texts A to D are extracts from war reports from various times:

Q. Identify the varieties of English and comment on significant linguistic features of the texts:

Text A

...notwithstanding the stubborn disposition of the enemy, our forces moved slowly ahead in an encircling movement

A company of enemy guns overlooking the western defile was destroyed, leaving that approach undefended and uncontested. Not rushing in to fill this gap was Hugo's first real mistake that day; we never gave him a chance to recover, pressing ever forward through the opening until our lines had shredded his at more than a dozen points. Our redoubtable foe was used to victory. He knew not how to handle what was now so patently the beginning of a decisive defeat. In a desperate bid to stave off the inevitable, he forced us to expend more and yet more... (middle of the 18th century)

Text B

...A thousand of the woollies came rushing at us with their spears, most of them big, brawny rogues with beatific smiles on their faces. Spears? Surely they had had reports of our prowess! Yet they seemed to be ready and anxious to die, filled with joy at the prospect of engaging us. We were no less anxious to accommodate them. The canvas covers of the machine guns were thrown off. The dreadful mechanical stuttering started up as they came in range. They dropped by the dozen, by the score, nay, by the hundred. Those few who survived drew hastily away and disappeared in confusion over the low hills some three hundred yards to the front and left of us. Never has victory been more complete or one-sided than this. The plains ahead of us were profusely spotted with those black bodies, most of them lying still, some twitching or moving about feebly. In such a climate death distends the belly with gases within minutes. The smell of putrefaction soon assailed our nostrils as the desert sun came up. Of our own number we had lost but nine, six to the wildly thrown spears of our foolish adversaries, and three when one of our powder cases mysteriously blew up...(early twentieth century)

Text C

... We beg to remind Your Grace, that the Rebel hath full many a Dowty Warrior among those in his Following, and that he hath so plumped up their Harts with the Venom of Sacrilege against thy most Sacred and Reuered Person, that we may not in the least hold to any expectation of Mercy, or of Sound Reason, or of the Spirit of Accommodation, should he, or should they, prevail, in this most Dire Struggle. The Fullest Possible preparations must be made without Delay; for, even as we write this, we learn that the Rebel doth March Forth southward, at the head of a Great and Terrible Armie of Fanatics... (seventeenth century)

Text D

... My motor started to misbehave again, giving me less than eighty percent power. The last thing I wanted was to encounter an enemy fighter, but luck was against me. To my left I saw a Hurricane slipping in and out of the clouds. The enemy pilot saw me at almost the same time. I was treated to a display of aerobatics as he looped and zoomed and twisted. I realised that he was frightened, so, with my spitting, coughing motor, I closed in to a point where I thought he would come out of his last loop. I waited for him to stop. Then I shot him down... (Translation from German records, mid-twentieth century)

IV

1. Many people have pointed out the absurdities of English spelling

Q. Write about the spelling of words in English. Give

reasons why attempts to reform it usually fail. Discuss the advantages and disadvantages of retaining traditional spelling.

2. If one is to talk at all about the rights and wrongs of a language, if one is to teach that language to foreigners, one must know what it is. One simply must have standards for it.

Q. Discuss the notion of 'correctness' in English with reference to its status among languages in the world today.

3. Some people object to phrases like 'au fait' (well-informed) or 'amour propre' (self esteem) in English. Yet English has been borrowing and absorbing foreign expressions for centuries. The use of French might cause pain to purists; but would they stop using words like 'chauvinist, 'large', 'difference' or 'calm' if they knew that they had been borrowed from France?

Q: More recent borrowings include words like intifada' and 'scenario'. Some people say that foreign words carry connotations somewhat different from those of English equivalents, and that they might be more suitable at certain times or in certain situations. Discuss.

The purpose of such questions and assignments is to provide a little background information to set up trains of thoughts in the student's mind. This is better than just giving a topic to write about.

Similar to these, but more extensive, is to give the student a long passage on some topic a day or two before asking him to write anything. The questions should then not be based on the passage; they should set up inferential channels derived from the passage. It should not matter, in this kind of question, if the student continues to refer to the passage when he writes. The memory is not tested here.

In line with the general tone of what has been said before in this thesis, namely, that intrinsic motivation is better than extrinsic motivation, and that writing should become intentional rather than merely performative, the focus should be moved away from the teacher, or assignment-giver, or examiner, to the student, so that his own thinking and impulse to communicate inform and propel his writing.

Suggestive and inferential exercises and questions are better than the 'topic' approach in vogue at present. Student expectations, the product of educational conditioning in the country, tend to perpetuate this approach. However, better approaches might exist. Some have been suggested and discussed in this study. Further thinking along these lines should help in making students more willing to write, more willing to revise and improve what they write, and eventually more motivated towards achieving some precision and grace in their writing in the second language.

This might help them to become better writers in their first language if they are interested in developing literary skills there as well. The general belief is that a writer cannot be truly creative in a second language, but this statement should be questioned, especially when one sees examples like Conrad or Azam.

In any case, in helping a person to write one should take cognisance of what is implied in the process of writing. At the same time it is recommended that no short-sighted limitations be placed on the functions of the brain. It is an organ that continues to surprise the observer in its ability to move beyond traditional axioms and cliches.

Chapter 10 Notes

1. Gould, Diyanni, Smith, *The Act of Writing,* McGraw-Hill, 1989, v-vi

2. Brown, C., and Zoellenr, R., *The Strategy of Composition,* Ronald Press, NY, 1968, viii

3. Ibid.

4. Azam, 1., *Literary Studies,* PFI, Islamabad, 1999-2000, 115

5. 5. Allen, D., and Parks, J., *Essential Rhetoric,* Houghton Mifflin, Boston, 1969,7

Chapter Eleven
Conclusion

The foregoing survey has taken the author in the following directions:

1. Most people in Pakistan are confined to the immediate and concrete in their thinking patterns because most of them are limited by the acquisition of only two language skills. The Pakistani culture is still basically a *talking* culture. It should become more of a *writing* one. A strong effort to improve national literacy figures should be undertaken immediately, because illiterate people are denied the language dimensions, and more significantly, the *mental abilities and attitudes,* associated with reading and writing. When illiteracy figures are overwhelming, as they are in Pakistan, they can affect social vision, temperament and development. It is not enough that the country has a small percentage of literate people. The literate outlook has to become dominant in the

mixture. At the moment the illiterate outlook is dominant. The recent official announcement that there would be universal primary education is gratifying, though this should have been done fifty years ago. High literacy in Urdu or other Pakistani languages would translate more readily into literacy in English. The language would then become more commonly understood and used. Its value as a 'utility' vehicle would become more evident. It would gradually lose its present elitist status. Resentment against it contributes in no small measure to its present unsatisfactory absorption, especially among poorer sections of the population. Badly taught, learnt under rejectionist pressures by the population, yet compulsory at all levels, what results is a series of compromises and escape tactics. It is suggested that the natural forces of linguistic usage in the world today, both in and outside Pakistan, have already decided that English is extremely important and that it will remain so for the foreseeable future. Everything should be done to improve all the skills in Pakistan, but particularly the skill of writing. The present programme for teacher orientation and training in the country is fragmented and vague. It suffers from inadequate follow-up procedures, and tends to be neutralised by apathy and low-morale.

2. When learning to write, a young child is not the beneficiary of the kind of positive reinforcement he receives when he is learning

how to speak. The atmosphere is perfectionist rather than encouraging, and he might receive a lot of negative criticism. Negative attitudes tend to develop from the beginning, and may remain with him throughout his life.

3. Current approaches in the teaching of writing focus on 'process' rather than 'product', and a reduction in the beginning of the 'punishment' associated with awkward syntax, spelling or punctuation. Creativity and natural expression take precedence over correctness. This is possible and desirable at school, and can be graded over several years. The same approach can be made with senior students in order to encourage communication in writing, but the whole thing has to be condensed into a much tighter time frame.

4. Different varieties of Pakistani English are taught at school in Pakistan. A few teachers think that these dialects are close enough to Standard English to be acceptable, but many know they are different. English is taught through Urdu or one of the regional languages in all vernacular schools, although most teachers who have a teaching certificate or diploma also have a working knowledge of the main developments in ELT. By far the most common way of beginning English is *via* Urdu, which is then used as a prop all the way through, even at the intermediate and degree levels. Passages for reading are heavily spotted with Urdu translations of difficult words and

ideas. However, Urdu has a different kind of grammar and cannot be used, for example, to explain articles, because it does not use articles itself. There is a nearly universal reliance on grammar and translation in the main systems in the country, where English is started in class six. Students are still required to translate from one language to the other, in both directions. Authorised syllabuses have not changed in concept (and hardly in content) for as long as the researcher can remember (1).

5. No recommendations with regard to methodology are made here. It is suggested that methodology, and all related matters, be taken up properly at a national level through mechanisms such as those proposed in Numbers 29 and 30. Transplanting methods and ideas from abroad does not seem to work in Pakistan. Yet it must be realised that the situation is unsatisfactory. There is no magic, blanket 'method' for the amelioration of these problems. Serious research is indicated into all aspects of the language teaching complex in Pakistan, the emphasis at all times being on conditions and realities in Pakistan. This could be undertaken at the centre proposed in Numbers 29 and 30

6. A Kaplan-style report on rhetorical patterns in Urdu is indicated, as suggested in chapter seven. A fairly large-scale analysis of several Urdu prose texts would need to be undertaken in conjunction with an analysis of Pakistani

writers of English. This could be done at the centre envisaged in Numbers 29 and 30

7. Learning to use the language in Pakistan is commonly considered less important than getting good marks in examinations. A variety of short-cuts are encountered. The most common are 'guess' papers provided by experienced publishers who have a high rate of success because not much imagination has been displayed by syllabus designers, paper-setters or examiners for the last fifty years. Set-piece answers and summaries are supplied by the same publishers. If a student learns enough of them by heart he can be fairly sure of passing because teachers and examiners do not take kindly to any kind of originality. Underpaid examiners with hundreds of papers to mark are not likely to want to think or to make judgements about anything out of the ordinary. One way of countering this gridlock is to change syllabuses every four years

8. Some senior students come through this system to the university level with very high marks, but are often unable to write a paragraph or even a few lines sufficiently close to Standard English to pass muster. English is still viewed as a subject to be studied rather than learnt

9. There is no sign of a willingness to change at any level, be it planning, curriculum design, teaching methodology or testing procedures.

The system has acquired a mindless, change-resistant momentum of its own

10. A few people might be found who consistently compartmentalise the languages they speak. However, most of the population is exposed to a randomly English-ised Urdu on one side and a strongly Urdu-ised English on the other. This language mixing is further reinforced at a social level in journalism, government documents, the electronic media and commercial activities. Yet when it comes to evaluating a senior student's performance in English there is a tendency to judge it in terms of Standard English, thus setting up unreasonable neuroses and inhibiting expression, especially in writing.

11. Remediation is uncertain, and the lapse rate can be high. Language patterns learnt (or mislearnt) at school tend to prevail over remedial efforts at the university level. However, some sort of remediation is desirable if standards are not to fall further

12. For those students who do not need a great deal of English, what little they manage to pick up through translation and rote-learning at the BA level might be enough, though it must be pointed out that English is required at a fairly advanced level for most MA courses, regardless of the subject. However, the first concern of this study is students aspiring for the MA (English) degree, as some of these will become future language teachers of the country. One

proposal is that the first semester of the MA course be devoted to refresher teaching of the four skills before embarking on the main course of study. The author's feeling is that because of the special difficulties of writing, a bridging course specifically for this skill also be made available as a summer course between the BA and MA (a similar course could be made available between the Intermediate and the BA). Since the whole of the English language cannot be re-taught at such points, a detailed comparative analysis should be made, focusing on common differences between Standard and Pakistani English. A few suggestions have been given (chapter three), but a great deal more is required. Some differences might be deemed acceptable in the context of this society, and not so far from Standard English as to cause communicational problems in the context of the world at large. Other differences might be judged to be so far from current international standards as to affect communication and hasten the process of linguistic isolation. The researcher has suggested some criteria (chapter three). However, careful validation is required at all stages in the process. This has not been attempted here. It falls under the purview of a centre such as that suggested in Numbers 29 and 30

13. Precision is unlikely at this stage in the development of English in Pakistan

14. Punitive attitudes with regard to language

should be changed. Ridiculing or punishing an individual for the language he uses can have a lasting effect on his communicational readiness. A person's language becomes part of the web of his personality.

15. Although many students get pass marks in English most of them really fail to learn how to use it in writing. The very considerable total national input of effort, resources and time seems doomed to failure, not in terms of getting degrees but in terms of language ability. In looking for causes it is possible to find fault with almost every component of the language educational process, i.e., with educational planning, teaching, syllabus design, social expectation, social exposure, student attitudes, treating English as a subject and giving very little time for it, misusing what little time there is, testing and evaluation, and perhaps, also with the very reasons and purposes for which English is taught/learnt in Pakistan. According to Gatenby(2), there is only one valid purpose in learning a second language, and that is to learn it fully and properly. Unfortunately, there is a tendency to be satisfied with approximations and partial acquisitions

16. Once the causes are identified and understood, remedies might become visible. For this, properly conducted surveys would need to be mounted, as suggested in Numbers 29 and 30

17. However, there is a tendency to persist with the old ways, regardless of their proven inefficiency

18. All the skills are important. In the world at large there are many different spoken dialects of English, but writing tends to be fairly standard, at least among the major groups of speakers. Without a doubt, spoken English needs to be improved in Pakistan: but Pakistani writing in English needs to be improved even more

19. Though this has not been established, writing might be useful as a means of developing mental maturity

20. A detailed analysis is required as to why, in a century and a half, English has failed to take hold in the country beyond its present unsatisfactory level. There is no single reason. There is a tendency to blame teachers, or students, or methods, or institutions, or the national curriculum, or parents, or social attitudes and expectations. The truth probably lies in an amalgam of these factors. They form an interlocking matrix of educational paralysis. The researcher has already discussed some of these points, but much more is required. Teaching cannot really be improved in such a highly charged *examination-and-marks* atmosphere, because all efforts are directed at getting high marks by whatever means possible

21. The reputation of an institution rests on the results it can produce, and it is thus likely to engage or support only those teachers who fit into the general pattern rather than those who work

for real acquisitions in language ability. Parents contribute strongly to the perpetuation of these attitudes. In a competitive society such as this one, where admission to prestige or professional institutions hinges on examination scores, they have no time to waste on scholarship for its own sake

22. This is quickly picked up and reinforced by students. Their interest in education first and last is directed towards acquiring degrees and high marks, and not towards acquiring workable language skills. If they can short-circuit the hard, boring and often unsuccessful drudgery of second language learning as demanded, and proffered, by the system, they will readily do s

23. Despite knowing all this, educational authorities past and present have tended to turn a blind eye on the widespread failure of English in Pakistan. Despite cogent, indeed urgent, arguments against treating a language as a subject to be studied rather than as a set of skills to be learnt, which have come down in linguistic theory across at least a century (3), they have succeeded in maintaining the status quo with the inertial help of school and college administrators and teachers. English is still a ʽone-period-a-day' subject in the school curriculum

24. With full knowledge that things are not likely to change in the foreseeable future, the author's interest has centred on ways and means of improving student writing at the university

level. This will have little impact on the national scene, but a teacher can only work within the environment of policies, facilities, systems and attitudes he finds around him. He is a follower of instructions, not a creator of policies or systems. Educational excellence is not always the primary concern of institutions, though a great deal of lip service is paid to it. Money, marks and gross numbers are usually more important. Private institutions are openly mercenary. Government institutions are plagued by the well-known stasis, neurosis and hierarchical jealousy of the bureaucracy. The researcher knows of no institution in Pakistan where English is researched or taught for its own sake, without the destructive intrusion of external factors

25. The failure of a quarter of a century of workshops run by key institutions with the help of foreign agencies for upgrading teacher skills in ELT in the country, also needs to be analysed. The expected 'trickle down' effect has not been realised. No improvement whatsoever can be seen in students reaching the university level. If anything, some slippage has occurred since the researcher's earlier involvement in these endeavours. Again, several reasons might be found. The overwhelming one is the in-built inertia of the system from top to bottom

26. Asking teachers to change their teaching approaches is hardly relevant when, in fact, they have no say in anything they do, and might be

summarily transferred to 'hardship' postings or lose their jobs for daring, like young Oliver, to ask for 'more', or to complain about, or challenge, the system. Whatever idealism they might bring to their profession in the beginning, they soon settle into a myopic torpor in line with their lowly position in the chain of command. Perhaps the focus of these workshops has been misdirected right from the beginning. Perhaps they should have concentrated more on policy makers and parents. If they are to continue with the teacher at the focal point, the alternative is to give him a significant measure of autonomy, and some of decision making, otherwise not much will be achieved

27. The author has suggested some remedies that might be applied at the university level. These are largely in line with current theory in applied linguistics with special reference to writing. It is too much to expect students engaged in a high level, full time course, to discover remedies and functions by themselves, so some guidance should be given, either in bridging courses, or in refresher courses which do not try to do too much, before they become graduate or post-graduate students, or continuously as an in-course feature, the emphasis being at all times on practice rather than theory, with no examination at the end

28. The author's personal, informal experience shows that some application in this direction is beneficial, even if it cannot guarantee absolute

precision or correctness. The effort should be organised and managed properly, but it should not be bureaucratised too much. The basic purpose is to generate self-confidence and pride in written expression, without constant correction, grammatical carping or evaluative tension. In fact, enrolment should be voluntary and students should be allowed to leave the course if they feel it is doing nothing for them. It should be a 'skills acquisition' rather than a 'subject study' course. The hope is that skills acquired in it will somehow be transferred to the main field of study, where they are so desperately required

29. The author is acutely aware of the fact that this study is insufficient as it stands. A great deal more is needed by way of analysis and validation at all points in the process. In order to promote language studies a centre is needed for language research in some university, like the National University of Modern Languages, well-equipped enough and influential enough to make an impact on language planning, syllabus designing and teaching approaches in the country. Such a university would need to have strong 'language' and 'skills' interests, rather than 'subject' ones

30. The obvious choice is the *National University of Modern Languages* because of (a), its federal location, and (b), its extensive and nearly exclusive preoccupation with languages. A cross-fertilisation of ideas among the different

languages taught in this institution, plus ways and means adapted from many lands, would do much to help. Some years ago, it was observed that Pakistani students learning other languages sometimes seemed to acquire more of those languages in two years, than they did of English in seven. *If true, this observation deserves the closest possible attention.* It will take time, but this university could work towards becoming a national clearing house of information on languages. Research conducted here would have the additional advantage of being rooted in real language-learning situations, thus avoiding some of the ivory-tower activity associated with academic research. Chipping away at the edges of the monolith will not help very much. National 'situation and needs assessment' surveys could provide a starting point for a point-to-point overhauling of the system. Guide lines for syllabus making, evaluation and validation could be suggested for use and consumption throughout the country. At some stage the centre could embark on materials production for the achievement of some degree of unanimity, if not of uniformity, for other centres of teaching. Imported materials are too expensive for local students, and are not always relevant to local needs. The idea should not be to impose systems and materials on other institutions, but to provide a helpful focal point of resources for teacher-training, language planning and language learning material for the rest of the country, so that poorly funded institutions and institutions in backward areas are not excluded from the general effort. At the moment the area-wise imbalances are excessive.

Of the forty-five to fifty per cent literate people in this society claimed in official figures, an estimated one half to one third go through to class eight or class ten. That means about a fifth of the country's population has had some teaching exposure to English, though in widely varying degrees. Regardless of how well or badly they learn it at school, about five to six million people use it quite a lot in some form or variety in their daily work, and certainly much more in writing than in speaking. The researcher heard a government clerk state that what little English he knew he had picked up on the job because he was forced to use it, also, that his school had taught him hardly anything, and that, too, wrongly. The lowliest car mechanic who has learnt his trade on the job since childhood and who has had no formal education, will have his sign-board, order-forms and receipt books written in English rather than in Urdu; And, if he insists on Urdu, he will simply use what passes for Urdu today, a mixed language with numerous English words written in the Urdu script. Regardless of which language he uses, his accounting will be done in the European rather than the Persian/Pakistani version of Arabic numerals. Nowadays one hardly sees such numerals anywhere. Like their Indic forebears, Arabic numerals go from west to east rather than from east to west, so the transition to the European version is not a difficult one. However, the real question here is not the ease of the transition but why that transition has taken place at all. The answer is that Urdu is taking into itself more and more of the English way of doing things at all levels. Pakistan could, perhaps, once be described as an 'English-speaking' nation. It might still be described as one such. But it is not a good 'English-writing' nation.

Baumgardner points out the 'all-pervasive' influence of English in Pakistan (4).This influence is entirely disproportionate to the numerical ratio of regular users within the total population. That it should be so reflects its status within the country. It also reflects its worldwide role. Numbers do not need to be quoted to assert that above the village level, nearly all significant decision making is done in English. In spite of patriotic endeavours to promote Urdu or the regional languages, it should be clear by now that English has not only retained its 'prestige' position, it has actually widened it. The trend is visible in the rapid proliferation of expensive, private English-medium schools in the country, most of them filled to bursting point with students. Some of them are 'English-medium' in name rather than in fact. Such are the language imperatives of the world today. In economics one talks about 'market forces' as factors said to work by themselves and which resist bureaucratic interference. Similar 'market forces', it is claimed, determine a society's linguistic climate regardless of theoretical considerations or bureaucratic tinkering, and, like the analogy in economics just given, strongly intrusive global interests also impinge on the process. There should be no apology for recognising the need to strengthen English; nor, at this stage in the history of the country, should there be a repetition of the misplaced patriotism that, in the early days, sought to weaken or abandon it.

Men speak in a cacophony of sounds. An estimated 7000 languages are spoken round the world, and each language is made up of numerous dialects with varying degrees of mutual intelligibility. Yet the human species is one and there seems to be no good reason why it should have so many ways of expressing itself. Modern linguistics teaches us that there are universal elements of grammar, though this can be disputed. All languages need some kind of noun-verb formation for their basic expression, and all major languages have ways of dealing with time, space, movement, interrogation, giving orders, instructing, declaring, supposing and supplying conditions. Again, all languages display an elaborate system of modification, and recognition of number. Because of these and other similarities it is possible for speakers of one language to learn another. There is the transference of universals from one mode to another.

However, learning another language is never easy. Years of training and exposure might result in a certain degree of adequacy, though rarely of total mastery. Any teacher of a second or foreign language will confirm the frustrations which arise in trying to effect that transference. The problems are compounded in an ever dwindling global environment in which speech communities are forced to interact with one another. Such are the imperatives of trade, travel, politics and diplomacy today, that the answer seems to lie in the evolution of a global form of communication with which most people can be comfortable.

We see different approaches to this. The two dominant languages in the world till not long ago were English and French. Both are notorious for their phonetic, orthographic and structural irregularities, English more so than French. Various attempts have been made to create languages artificially. This is probably less difficult than it seems to be. The essential elements of human communication are already known. It becomes a question of deciding on a grammar and defining a set of words and utterances within a regular framework. Since there is no real correlation between a word and the thing it refers to, almost any sound will do for any object or idea. It should be possible to keep the vocabulary simple, monosyllabic and easy to pronounce. It should be possible to make the grammar systematic. The most famous example is Esperanto, and one will still find people in many countries who endorse it for its simplicity and ease of learning. Nevertheless Esperanto, as with all other artificial languages, has failed to become a widely used, international reality.

Given the observation that people would not ascribe to a language which had not grown out of a culture, and given the fact that a language without a real, human, cultural content was unnatural and empty, attempts were made to modify known languages so that they would become more acceptable to others. At the beginning of the twentieth century the world had English and French, spoken in what are known as the Anglophone and Francophone countries. However, these were colonies, and there was a lot of resentment against both the masters and their languages.

French faded as a serious contender between the two world wars. English lasted longer, but it, too, might have faded in the aftermath of the second world war when Britain's position declined sharply together with its disengagement from the colonies, had it not been for the dramatic political and economic rise of a much larger group of English speaking people, the Americans. However, even before the war it was recognised that if English were to become the international lingua franca it might be good to cleanse it of its colonial connotations and to rationalise its wayward grammar and spelling. Shaw's observations on spelling are well known. Less well known is that a man called Zacharias was asked to modify English (hence to be called Anglica to make it neutral and non-colonial) in the nineteen thirties. That attempt came to an end with his death and the commencement of hostilities in World War II.

At the moment nothing is being done to modify English or to make it more acceptable to others. There was some talk of offering it to the world as an international auxiliary language some years ago, to be used as much and in whatever way it might be needed by other speech communities. That movement seems to have faded. Linguistics has taught us that efforts to direct the process of change in a language or to preserve its purity usually fail, and that the 'market forces' of communication are the ultimate determiners of communication.

It may be argued that there are new and insidious ways of colonising the world through economic globalisation, preparing the ground for it by flooding the world with undoubtedly well-made cinematic, video, television and radio reflections (though often distorted ones) of English speaking culture, world news broadcasts in English, dress designs, catchy pop tunes and entertainment likely to appeal to the younger generation. There is a sustained message through subtle and unsubtle themes, suggesting that these are the best things to emulate. The new wave is the American-English culture, and its sheer mass and momentum seem to be taking it on the road to success. It encounters sporadic resistance from older people who cling to their memories. Younger people from Papua to Columbia are hardly aware of the assault, as they sit down to a breakfast of corn-flakes, read Mickey Mouse comic books, and eagerly absorb the endless projection of American values in films and TV shows (5).

Like it or not, English is already the language of international aviation, banking, commerce and diplomacy. Most of the world's publications in science and technology are in English, regardless of where the research and development is done. The greatest libraries are found in the English-speaking world, and they stock material on every conceivable aspect of modern living. A great deal of work is being done and a great deal of literature is being produced. Other languages are losing ground by default. English is taught as a foreign or second language all round the world, and *English Language Teaching* has evolved into a full-fledged discipline. No parallel discipline exists for any other language, the teaching of which tends to be put under some general head like *Applied Linguistics.* In some countries such as the Philippines and Nigeria it is practically used as the first language, while in some South Asian countries it is the joint official language with the dominant local claimant. In countries such as Iran, medical and engineering students do their reading in English, even if they write their examination answers in the local language. A hundred years from now Chinese or Hindi might take over as the dominant world language. Nobody knows. But for the next fifty years, at least, no serious rival is likely to emerge, such is the growing spread of English today, exceeding anything Latin or Sanskrit might have had in ancient times.

The fear is that if Anglo-Saxon domination continues for another few decades, English might push several or all other languages off the planet. The trend is not visible today. Most people would scoff at the notion that their own language could possibly disappear. They would do well to remember that some great and famous historical languages died out when their utility level fell below that of other claimants, when they were exhausted, or when they broke up into smaller languages. A language lives or dies in proportion to the economic, industrial, military, intellectual and artistic vigour of the culture that supports it. When a culture allows itself to become unprogressive, lazy, passive and non-inventive, the language which expresses it is likely to find itself at a disadvantage. English might first drive out many other tongues, but in the process it might itself break up into derived languages round the globe. We are in the midst of a process at this point, and the end results are not clear. There are fissiparous trends in dialects of English everywhere, but there are also unifying trends in media dissemination and in the greatly increased traffic between people. It remains to be seen which trends will emerge the stronger.

Recommendations:

1. Rahman and Baumgardner have done well to analyse and describe trends in Pakistan. The researcher's plea is for much more of the same, and that some considered judgement be given as to how far the process

of indigenisation should be allowed to go unchecked. Linguistic change is a fact of life, but it is also desirable not to let it run wild. The researcher started his thesis on the premise that Pakistani English is at present quite far from current international models, which are themselves by no means absolute, and that it seems unfair to students that they should learn one variety of English only to be judged in terms of other models. The shock for students reaching the MA level when they discover that the English they have been using all their lives is now deemed unacceptable is disheartening. Many of them then resort to undesirable ways of passing examinations. This does considerable harm to their self-image and confidence. Some accommodation is required. Some criteria need to be determined.

2. At the same time the researcher has suggested that what happens within the nation should not be the only criterion for judging the appropriacy of Pakistani trends, because English is also the nation's link with the world. In establishing criteria, both perspectives have to be kept in mind. Baumgardner seems fully accepting of Pakistanisms like 'affectee', 'ad-hocism', 'de-load', 'history-sheeter', 'botheration', and others (p 43-47). Certainly, expressions like these do not cause any problems for users of English within the country. Would they or would they not cause communicational problems for users of English outside the country? The researcher

does not know[7], but he suggests that this is something that needs to be analysed and judged in determining criteria for a national standard, if such a thing is possible.

3. With regard to literature, the original purpose was to introduce students to examples of literary excellence so that they would have impeccably 'English' models in thought and writing to draw upon. A secondary purpose was, of course, the dissemination of English culture. A tertiary one, no doubt, was to save the souls of the natives. The focus was supposed to be on understanding and on creative critical appreciation. In fact, since the nineteen sixties or even earlier, encapsulated opinions as provided in conveniently juxtaposed collections *{Cole's Notes, Cliff's Notes, B.R Malik's Notes, Urdu Bazaar* publications, etc)* have tended to be learnt by heart for exact regurgitation in examinations, a practice that has hardened over time. Textual analysis and the flexible use of the English language are dreams long forgotten.

    Whatever purposes the British might have had in introducing English literature to this region, it can only be justified in Pakistan today if it helps in mastering the language. As an aid to learning the language, English literature as it is taught, learnt and examined in Pakistan has little value. Studying good writing or learning it by heart does not seem to result in an ability to write well. Nor, frankly, can much use be seen for models of Middle English or Early Modern

English writing, except for students trying to specialise in the history of English literature. The author still gets the odd student who thinks that he has written poetry because he has used words like 'thee' and 'thou', regardless of the banality of the thought. The whole question of classical literature as an accessory to learning modern English needs to be re-examined urgently.

Not much seems to have changed from a hundred years before the researcher sat his MA examination till now, forty years later. The standard MA syllabus contained, and still contains, Chaucer, Spenser, Donne, Shakespeare and Milton. While they are interesting, it is difficult to see how they can contribute to the language learning process. Shakespeare would, in fact, reinforce modern Pakistani solecisms like 'Amina married *with* her cousin', or double comparatives like 'Jamil is *more better* than Aslam at playing tennis'. The teacher might tell his student that such expressions are wrong, only to have the student show him examples taken from the writings of one of the most revered names in English letters.

It is time to question the wisdom or pedagogical utility of hurling students who have just staggered out of their BA examinations with very little ability to express themselves in modern English, into an ocean of Middle and Early Modern English. There is a tendency to approach writers of English literature with an attitude of awe, as though they are rare creatures endowed with timeless morality or wisdom, and not just ordinary, fallible men and women who have learnt how to express themselves in their own language unusually well. The assertion here is that it is less important to learn a few facts about Chaucer or Donne than it is to be able to use modern English for whatever purposes Pakistanis need to use it, today and in the near future. The plea here is that all planning be done within a strictly utilitarian framework, and that the end purpose of language ability be kept firmly in mind. This should be done as an interim measure. At a later stage, perhaps half a century on, the luxury of 'useless' knowledge might be welcomed into the language curriculum, but not at this point. Yet people still look for justifications for continuing with the old, 'tried and true' patterns. The British brought in their literature for several reasons, basically to create an English mind-set and to push local culture out through a combination of lofty ridicule and studied disuse. Can any of those reasons be relevant to Pakistan today? The basic proposition must be reiterated strongly. Literature has a place, but a subordinate one. And the term 'English' literature is wide enough to include all good writing in English, wherever it comes from, including this sub-continent with special reference to this part of it.

4. Writing seems to have fallen by the way in the national effort to learn English. It requires special attention. In many ways it is the most

difficult and most sensitive of the skills. The author has suggested some approaches in this study. In the main, these are based on his own experience, though they have direct reference to, and confirmation from, current practice in other parts of the world. However, a lot of this has been informal, fitted into small gaps in the overall effort of students to cover their massive courses in literature, suggested in extra assignments, or pursued in special sessions outside the normal course schedule. Of necessity, the effort and its evaluation have been ad-hoc and fragmentary. Even so, the results have been gratifying on occasion. It is suggested that much more could be done in an organised manner, and that the matter is serious enough to require urgent consideration.

Afterthoughts:

English teaching in Pakistan is still disordered, misdirected and wasteful. Nothing significant has happened since partition. No recent innovation in language teaching is visible in the vast mass and bulk of schools round the country, though there may be a few exceptions in big urban centres. By and large, educational planners and teachers have refused to take advantage of sound theory and of promising, if not entirely proven, practice. Learner-centred methods that focus on the student's hopes and capabilities, are lost in the scramble for marks. Creativity, the very essence of language, is drowned in stereotyped note giving, answer-book conformity and predictable testing procedures.

Language deficiencies generated and hardened at school act as a stumbling block to performance at higher levels. Advanced studies in literature, in which many related interests in sociology, psychology, philosophy and aesthetics need to be discussed in a painless flow of language, are hampered because that language is not there. Standards tend to remain low. There is a lot of wastage of student effort, not to mention psychological problems, demoralisation and recourse to undesirable methods to circumvent those deficiencies rather than to address them.

An important skill among the language skills in academic pursuits is writing. Students who are able to understand quite a lot when others speak, or who can speak reasonably well when they need to, are found to be diffident and evasive when it comes to writing. Other skills cannot be ignored, but this skill demands specific treatment, partly as an adjunct to other skills, and partly as a process in and of itself

The researcher continues to believe that speaking variations do not matter very much provided an acceptable level of communication is maintained, and that despite their marked accent Pakistani speakers of English can interact without much strain with other speakers of English round the world. However, there is little justification for excessive deviation in writing. As far as possible, English writing in Pakistan should be brought in line with that of the dominant groups of English users in the world today.

Chapter 11 Notes

1. The reader will be surprised to learn that *Goodbye Mr Chips,* which was current thirty years ago, is still found at the intermediate level. It alternates with *The Prisoner of Zenda,* another very old component of the intermediate syllabus. The researcher has sat at some 'syllabus review' sessions; in many institutions they amount to little more than shuffling a limited number of texts around, often at the whim of senior members of the committees.

2. Gatenby, E., "Reasons for Failure to Learn a Foreign Language," *English Language Teaching Selections* 1, ed. Lee,W., Oxford, London, 1970,6

3. Actually, much more than a century: this is what Locke had to say about language learning in the *seventeenth* century: *'Languages were not made by rules or art, but by accident and the common use of people. And he that will speak them well has no other rule but that, nor anything to trust but his own memory...'* The prescience is remarkable, but this observation made as little impact on teaching practices in his own age as similar ones do on ours (in Gatenby, E., "Conditions for Success in Language Learning", Ibid., 12). Prescriptive grammar has displayed remarkable tenacity in the face *of* linguistic theory. It is still very much at the centre of language teaching in Pakistan. As suggested in chapter one, this is by default, because other models of grammar are either too permissive and vague, or too complex

and mathematical, to help in the process of learning a language, especially the early part of it.

4. Baungardner, R., "The Indigenisation of English in Pakistan", in *The English Language in Pakistan,* ed., Baumgardner, R., Oxford, 1993, 41. In line with descriptive models, Baumgardner's approach is informative and tolerant. No judgement is implied. However, the researcher feels that some processing and guiding is desirable, especially in writing. Pakistan has already drifted too far from international norms in this skill.

5. Local newspapers contribute to the process. The most widely read English newspaper in the country is *The News.* It has a Saturday supplement for children which projects American cartoon characters like *Mickey Mouse* and *Donald Duck.* Likewise, nearly all the cartoon strips *(Peanuts, Blondie, Robot Man, Born Loser, Li'l Abner, Popeye, Dennis the Menace,* etc.,) shown in local newspapers are of American origin. So are the language exercises in crosswords (which require a knowledge of American history, spelling, idiom, slang, culture and geography), scrabble and cryptograms. Other people, especially in the third world, find it much easier to use such ready-made facilities than to sit down and match them in the local idiom. The Americans have worked hard for the projection of their culture, and have done it attractively and efficiently. Their influence is not confined to backward countries. It is also found in 'culturally proud' countries like France and Germany; and even

in the cradle and former bastion of the language, Great Britain. Since the early nineteen sixties, popular songs have been sung in a pseudo-American accent in Britain. Changes might also be noted in the British pronunciation of words like 'schedule'(from 'shedule' to 'skedule'), 'kilometre' (from *ki*lomeeter" to 'ke*lah*meter'), 'address'(from 'er*dress*' to '*ad*ress'), 'harass' (from '*har*ass' to 'har*ass),* among many others. It makes no difference. Human flexibility is usually enough to accommodate such changes. The local complaint is, of course, that these changes and uncertainties emanating from the two large centres of the language are making things difficult for other people trying to learn English. "What is English?' is the anguished cry of the second language learner. Unfortunately, we are not in a position to give him clear answers.

Glossary

1. *behaviourism*: people with a scientific bent of mind stated (perhaps overstated) that, if psychology were to be treated as a science, it could allow itself to deal with only those manifestations of behaviour that could be observed. Speculation about the unseen inner working of the brain was frowned upon. This was the dominant school of psychology in America for much of the twentieth century, although it also had adherents in other parts of the world, including Pakistan. The behavioural approach is by no means dead today, but it is now generally more willing than before to make grudging concessions for mental activity that cannot be observed. Some people feel that an approach that ignores the inner working of the brain (which is a large area for plausible speculation) just because it cannot see or measure it, is unduly restrictive and cannot be called truly scientific.

2. *LAD/LAS*: these are acronyms for Language Acquisition Device and Language Acquisition System. The assumption is that without instruction infants learn the languages spoken in their environment at their own speed and according to some innate agenda. In fact, meddling with that agenda might disturb it, so it is best to let it work in its own way. *Acquisition* is considered to be different from *learning* in that it proceeds naturally, whereas learning requires instruction and deliberate effort. The natural skills are said to be the 'oracy' skills of listening and speaking. The relatively artificial skills,

namely, the 'literacy' skills of reading and writing; are said to require a lot of hard work and instruction

3. *pscyholinguistics*: a study of language from a psychological point of view. Actually, almost anything you one think of comes under the purview of psychology, so this area of linguistics is not well defined. Mostly it has to do with acquiring (or learning) a language, thinking and language, the evolution of human language (which includes studies of animal communication) and the effects of language on people

4. *sociolinguistics:* language has obvious social implications since it is used for communicating with other people. As with psycholinguistics this is also a wide field. Among other things, it deals with interactional aspects of language, communication, dialects, registers, modes of language, culture and the role of language in society.

5. *The Sapir-Whorf hypothesis* : this hypothesis did not fit very neatly into the assumptions made by the early writers in pscyholinguistics, namely that there is a universal grammar, that all languages are essentially the same and that children pick up the tools of language easily because the concepts required for understanding and accepting the terms they hear spoken by people around them already exist in their minds. In other words, a child does not need to be taught the meaning of, say, 'eat,' because the word when he hears it is readily associated with some innate concept in his brain. Whorf, whose name is more commonly coupled with this hypothesis than that of Sapir, has probably been misrepresented by

later writers. It is interesting to speculate how different languages might guide, define, promote and limit the thinking patterns of their users. Do we look at similarities or at differences, or do we admit that while human beings certainly share much in their understanding of the world, their perceptions in some areas might be different? The Sapir-Whorf hypothesis should not be dismissed too readily. It is interesting, also, to speculate that different kinds of writing affect the psychology of the writer in some way. Writing makes a kind of 'map' of reality for those who use it or read it. For example, does a system that moves from right to left have a different psychological effect from a system that moves from left to right? Or down and up, or up and down? Of interest would be the following questions: (1) Do Urdu speakers and writer of Urdu see the world significantly differently from people who speak and write English? (2) Does an additional ability to write in English make a psychological difference to someone who already knows how to write in Urdu? (3) Would the psychology of a person who knows how to write in English but not how to write in his first language, be different from that of a person who knows how to write in both? (4) Would the kind of script that a person uses have any effect on his way of looking at the world? Many other questions can be found in combinations of these elements, and it would be interesting to extend Whorf's ideas to written forms of languages, which have obvious differences in direction and approach. Some writing scripts separate sounds in an analytical framework, some synthesize sounds. Some do not represent sounds but ideas.